MARC_____

ITALIAN

with Local Tips

WORLD LEISURE MARKETING

CONTENTS

CONTENTS

Cover photo: IFA Bilderteam / Förster, Munich
p. 68, 69: Ali Mitgutsch "Let's go to the Sea", "All around my town"
© Ravensburger Buchverlag Otto Maier GmbH

1st English edition 1997 © Mairs Geographischer Verlag, Ostfildern Germany
© based on PONS Reisewörterbuch Italienisch
Copyright Ernst Klett Verlag für Wissen und Bildung GmbH, Stuttgart 1992
edited by Barbara Huter, revised by Serena Kästel
Editorial: Ernst Klett Verlag für Wissen und Bildung, Stuttgart;
Mairs Geographischer Verlag, Ostfildern; Barbara Pflüger, Stuttgart
Cover design: Thienhaus / Wippermann, Hamburg
Printed in Italy

Pronunciation

On the whole Italian is pronounced exactly as it is written. Normally, the stress falls on the penultimate syllable (ristorante, venire, giornale), but there are a few exceptions to this rule. These are marked with a dot under the syllable which should be stressed (eg piccolo, giovane).

Pronunciation guide

● when two vowels are juxtaposed each one is clearly articulated: E-uropa

vowels

a, e, and o are 'hard vowels', i and u are soft vowels. The following examples will help you to pronounce them correctly:	
a	as in art
e	as in pet
i	like the ea in eat
o	as in hot
u	like the oo in boot

consonants

b, d, f, l, m, n, p, t and v have more or less the same sound as in English. Double consonants are clearly emphasized: bel-lo		
c, cc	as in "cat" before a consonant or before the vowels "a", "o" and "u"	classe banco casa
	pronounced "ch" as in "church" before an "e" or an "i"	accento dieci
ch, cch	like the "c" in "cat"	che, pacchi
ci, cci	pronounced "ch" as in "church" before "a", "o" and "u"	ciao! cioccolata

g, gg	as in "good" before a consonant or before the vowels "a", "o" and "u"	**g**rande **g**ondola
	pronounced like a "j" as in "jam" before "e" and "i"	**g**ente o**gg**i
gh	as in "good"	**gh**iaccio
gi, ggi	pronounced like a "j" as in "jam"	man**gi**are
gl	pronounced like a "y" preceded by a short "l"; it sounds like the "li" in "pavilion"	fi**gl**io
gn	pronounced like an "n" followed by a "y"; it sounds like the "ni" in "onion" or the "gn" in "cognac"	ba**gn**o
h	is never pronounced	**h**o
qu	as in "queen"	ac**qu**a
r	is a lightly rolled "r"	ma**r**e
s	pronounced "s" as in "sun" at the beginning of a word (except when followed by the consonants listed below) and when it is a double "ss".	**s**ole **s**era
	pronounced like the "s" in "rose" when it falls between two vowels and at the beginning of a word before the consonants "b, d, g, l, m, n, v".	ro**s**a
sc	as in "scratch" before a consonant or the vowels "a", "o" and "u"	**sc**rivere **sc**usi
	pronounced "sh" as in "ship" before "e" or "i"	pe**sc**e, u**sc**ita
sch	as in "school"	I**sch**ia
sci	pronounced "sh" as in "ship" before "a", "o" and "u"	la**sci**are **sci**opero

Masculine or feminine?

As a general rule, nouns which end in the letter **-o** are masculine (eg **il** bagnin**o** – lifeguard) and nouns ending in **-a** are feminine (eg **la** cas**a** – house). There are a few exceptions to this rule and in these cases the gender is indicated (eg **la** man**o** f – hand; **la** canzon**e** f – song).

The Italian Alphabet

A	a	[ah]	J	j	[ee loongo]	S	s	[esse]
B	b	[bee]	K	k	[cappa]	T	t	[tee]
C	c	[chee]	L	l	[elle]	U	u	[oo]
D	d	[dee]	M	m	[emme]	V	v	[voo]
E	e	[eh]	N	n	[enne]	W	w	[voo doppio]
F	f	[effe]	O	o	[o]	X	x	[ics]
G	g	[jee]	P	p	[pee]	Y	y	[ipsilon]
H	h	[acca]	Q	q	[coo]	Z	z	[dzetta]
I	i	[ee]	R	r	[erre]			

Abbreviations

adj.	adjective	aggettivo
adv.	adverb	avverbio
s.th.	something	qualcosa
f.	feminine	femminile
s.b.	somebody	(a) qualcuno
m.	masculine	maschile
pl.	plural	plurale
qc	something	qualcosa
qlc	someone	qualcuno

Making friends

Yes.	Sì.
No.	No.
Please.	Per favore.
Thank you.	Grązie.
You're welcome.	Prego!
Pardon?	Come dice?
Of course.	Certo.
Agreed!	D'accordo!
OK!	Va bene!
Excuse me.	Scusi!
Just a minute, please.	Un momento, prego!
I'd like ...	Vorrei ...
Is there ...?/Are there ...?	C'è/Ci sono ...?
Help!	Aiuto!

Who?	Chi?
Who ... to?	A chi?
What?	Che cosa?
Which?	Quale?
How much?	Quanto/Quanta?
How many?	Quanti/Quante?
How?	Come?
Why?	Perchè?
What ... for?	A che cosa?
Where?	Dove?
Where ... from?	Da dove?
Where ... to?	Dove?
When?	Quando?
How long?	Per quanto tempo?

GREETINGS

GOOD MORNING/ AFTERNOON!	BUON GIORNO!
Good evening.	Buọna sera!
Hello/Hi!	Ciạo!
What's your name?	Come si chiạma?/Come ti chiạmi?

MY NAME'S ...	MI CHIẠMO ...
Pleased to meet you.	Sono lieto/lieta di conoscerla.
May I introduce you? This is ...	Le posso presentare ...
Mrs X.	la signora X.
Miss X.	la signorina X.
Mr X.	il signor X.
my husband.	mio marito.
my wife.	mia mọglie.
my son.	mio fịglio.
my daughter.	mia fịglia.
my brother.	mio fratello.
my sister.	mia sorella.
my boyfriend/girlfriend.	il mio amico/la mia amica.
How are you?	Come sta?/Come stai?
Fine thanks. And you?	Bene, grạzie. E Lei/tu?
Where are you from?	Di dov'ẹ Lei?/ Di dove sei tu?
I'm from ...	Sono di ...

Are you on your own?	È/Sei solo/a?
How old are you?	Quanti anni ha/hai?
I'm thirty-nine.	Ho trentanove anni.

YES, PLEASE / SÌ, GRAZIE

Could you do me a favour?	Le posso chiedere un favore?
May I?	Permette?
Can you help me, please?	Mi può aiutare, per favore?

THANK YOU! / GRAZIE!

Thank you very much.	Tante grazie.
Yes, thank you.	Grazie, molto volentieri.
Thank you. The same to you.	Grazie, altrettanto.
That's very kind of you, thank you.	Molto gentile, grazie.
With pleasure.	Con piacere.
Fine!	Magnifico!
Thank you very much ... for your help. for your trouble.	Grazie ... del Suo aiuto. della Sua premura.
Don't mention it.	Non c'è di che! / Prego!
You're welcome.	Non c'è di che! / Prego!

I'M SORRY! / SCUSI!

I'm so sorry!	Mi dispiace tanto.
I didn't mean it.	Non intendevo questo.
What a pity!	Peccato! / Che peccato!

PARDON? / COME DICE?

I don't understand.	Non capisco.
Would you repeat that, please?	Ripetalo / Lo ripeti, per favore.
Would you speak a bit more slowly, please?	Per favore, parli/parla più piano.
I understand.	Capisco.
I only speak a bit of ...	Parlo solo un po' di ...

Have you got any plans for tomorrow?	Hai già un programma per domani?
Shall we go together?	Ci andiamo insieme?
When shall we meet?	A che ora ci incontriamo?
Are you married?	Sei sposato/sposata?
Have you got a boyfriend/ a girlfriend?	Hai un ragazzo/una ragazza?
I've been looking forward to seeing you all day.	Ti ho aspettato tutto il giorno con impazienza.
You've got beautiful eyes!	Hai degli occhi stupendi!
I've fallen in love with you.	Mi sono innamorato/innamorata di te.
I love you, too.	Io pure ti amo.
I love you!	Ti amo!
I'm sorry, but I'm not in love with you.	Mi dispiace, ma non ti amo.
Your place or mine?	Andiamo a casa mia o a casa tua?
I would like to sleep with you.	Vorrei andare a letto con te.
I don't want to.	Non ne ho voglia.
I don't want to.	Non voglio.
Stop at once!	Smettila!
Only with a condom!	Però solo col preservativo!
Do you have a condom?	Ne hai preservativi?

Just good friends?

"Amico/amica" means *friend* eg *"This is my friend Fred"* *("Questo e il mio amico Fred")* whereas *"ragazzo/ragazza"* *(literally boy/girl)* means *boyfriend* or *girlfriend*. The Italian equivalent to *"partner"* is *"compagno/compagna"*.

"Permesso"

In Italy, when you visit the home of someone you don't know, it is polite to say *"permesso"* before entering. This means something like *"may I come in"* or *"excuse me"*.

Can I take you home?	La/Ti posso accompagnare a casa?
Please leave now!	Per favore, adesso vạttene!
Please leave me alone!	Mi lasci in pace, per favore!
Go away/Get lost!	Sparisci!

GOODBYE!   ARRIVEDERCI!

See you soon!	A presto!
See you later!	A più tardi!
See you tomorrow!	A domani!
Good night!	Buona notte!
Cheerio!	Ciạo!
Have a good journey.	Buon viạggio!

CONGRATULATIONS!   AUGURI!

All the best!	Tante belle cose!
Happy birthday!	Tanti auguri per il compleạnno.
Good luck!	Buon lavoro!/Buona fortuna!
Get well soon!	Buona guarigiọne!
Have a good holiday!	Buone feste!

"In bocca al lupo!"

This literally means *"into the mouth of the wolf"*. It is an ironic expression used to wish someone luck, usually before they have to face a sticky situation or an ordeal of some kind. The English equivalent would be *"break a leg"*. If the person you have said it to is optimistic about the outcome, he will reply *"E crepi il lupo!"* which means *"and may the wolf die a painful death"*.

11

WHERE IS ...?

Excuse me, where's ...?	Scusi signore/signora/signorina, dov'è ...?
Could you tell me how to get to ..., please?	Mi potrebbe dire come si arriva a ..., per favore?
I'm sorry, I don't know.	Mi dispiace, non lo so.
Which is the quickest way to ... ?	Qual è la strada più breve per ...?
How far is it to ... ?	Quanto ci vuole per andare a ...?
It's a long way. It's not far	È lontano. Non è lontano.
Go straight on. Turn left. Turn right.	Vada diritto. Vada a sinistra. Vada a destra.
The first/second street on the left/right.	La prima/seconda strada a sinistra/a destra.

Cross ...
  the bridge.
  the square.
  the street.
	Attraversi ...
	  il ponte.
	  la piazza.
	  la strada.

Then ask again.	Poi chieda un'altra volta.
You can't miss it..	Non si può sbagliare.

You can take ...
  the bus.
  the tram.
  the tube.
	Può prendere ...
	  l'autobus.
	  il tram.
	  la metropolitana.

"favoloso!"

You can express your joy, enthusiasm or liking for something or someone with the following adjectives:

favoloso	(great)
fenomenale	(unbelievable, amazing)
stupendo	(fantastic)
eccezionale	(amazing, extraordinary)
ottimo	(excellent)
splendido	(brilliant, splendid)
meraviglioso	(wonderful)

THE TIME

TIME	L'ORA

What time is it?

It's (about) …

- 🕒 3 o'clock.
- 🕒 5 past 3.
- 🕒 10 past 3.
- 🕒 quarter past 3.
- 🕒 half past 3.
- 🕒 quarter to 4.
- 🕐 5 to 4.

Che ore sono?

Sono (circa) …

- le tre.
- le tre e cinque.
- le tre e dieci.
- le tre e un quarto.
- le tre e mezza.
- le quattro meno un quarto.
- le quattro meno cinque.

What time?/When?

At one o'clock.
At two o'clock.
At about 4 o'clock.
In an hour's time.
In two hours' time.
Not before 9 a.m.
After 8 p.m.
Between three and four.

A che ora?/Quando?

All'una.
Alle due.
Verso le quattro.
Fra un'ora.
Fra due ore.
Non prima delle nove del mattino.
Dopo le otto di sera.
Tra le tre e le quattro.

How long?

For two hours.
From ten to eleven.
Till five o'clock.

Per quanto tempo?

Per due ore.
Dalle dieci alle undici.
Fino alle cinque.

Since when?

Since 8 a.m.
For half an hour.

Da quando?

Fin dalle otto del mattino.
Da mezz'ora.

about noon/midday	verso mezzogiorno
at lunchtime	a mezzogiorno
at night	di notte
at the weekend	a fine settimana
during the day	di giorno
during the morning	la mattina
every day	ogni giorno
every day, daily	tutti i giorni, giornaliero
every half hour	ogni mezz'ora
every hour, hourly	ogni ora
every other day	ogni due giorni
from time to time	di tanto in tanto
in a fortnight's time	fra quindici giorni
in the afternoon	il pomeriggio
in the evening	di sera
in the morning	la mattina (presto)
last Monday	lunedì scorso
next year	l'anno prossimo
now	ora
on Sunday	domenica
sometimes	a volte
soon	presto
ten minutes ago	dieci minuti fa
the day after tomorrow	dopo domani
the day before yesterday	l'altro ieri
this week	questa settimana
to recently	recentemente
today	oggi
tomorrow	domani
tomorrow evening	domani sera
tomorrow morning	domattina
within a week	entro una settimana
yesterday	ieri

THE DATE | **DATA E ETÀ**

What's the date (today)?	Quanti ne abbiamo oggi?
Today's the first of May (May the first).	Oggi è il primo maggio.

> The date is always given with cardinal numbers: *"il due agosto"* – *"the second of August"* (literally: *"the two of August"*). The only exception is with the first of the month when the ordinal number *"primo"* is used: *"il primo agosto"* – *"the first of August"*.

DAYS OF THE WEEK	I GIORNI DELLA SETTIMANA
Monday	lunedì
Tuesday	martedì
Wednesday	mercoledì
Thursday	giovedì
Friday	venerdì
Saturday	sabato
Sunday	domenica

MONTHS OF THE YEAR	I MESI		
January	gennaio	July	luglio
February	febbraio	August	agosto
March	marzo	September	settembre
April	aprile	October	ottobre
May	maggio	November	novembre
June	giugno	December	dicembre

SEASONS	LE STAGIONI		
spring	primavera	autumn (fall)	autunno
summer	estate *f*	winter	inverno

HOLIDAYS	GIORNI FESTIVI
New Year's Day	Capodanno
Epiphany	L'Epifania
Carnival	Carnevale
Mardi Gras	Martedì grasso
Ash Wednesday	Mercoledì delle ceneri
Maundy Thursday	Giovedì Santo
Good Friday	Venerdì Santo
Easter	Pasqua
Easter Monday	Lunedì dell' Angelo/Pasquetta
April 25th	Liberazione
May 1st / May Day	Festa del lavoro
Corpus Christi	Corpus Domini
The Assumption (August 15th)	Assunzione, Ferragosto
All Saints Day (November 1st)	Ognissanti
Immaculate Conception (December 8th)	Immacolata Concezione
Christmas Eve	Vigilia di Natale
Christmas	Natale
Christmas Day	Il giorno di Natale
Boxing Day	Santo Stefano
New Year's Eve	San Silvestro

WEATHER

What's the weather going to be like today?	Che tempo farà oggi?
It's going to stay fine/bad.	Rimane bello/brutto.
It's going to get warmer/colder.	Si sta facendo più caldo/freddo.
It's going to rain/snow.	Pioverà/Nevicherà.
It's cold/hot.	Fa freddo/caldo.
It's close/humid.	C'è afa.
What's the temperature today?	Quanti gradi abbiamo oggi?
It's twenty degrees centigrade.	Abbiamo una temperatura di 20 gradi.

air	aria
black ice	strade ghiacciate
changeable	variabile
climate	il clima
cloud	nuvola
cloudy	nuvoloso
cold	freddo
drought	siccità
flooding, floods	l'alluvione *f*
fog	nebbia
frost	gelo
heat	caldo
high tide	alta marea
hot	caldo, bollente
humid	afoso
lightning	il fulmine
low tide	bassa marea
powder snow	la neve farinosa
rain	pioggia
rainy	piovoso
snow	la neve
sun	il sole
sunny	soleggiato, assolato
temperature	temperatura
thunder	tuono
thunderstorm	il temporale
warm	caldo
weather forecast	le previsioni metereologiche
weather report	bollettino meteorologico
wet	bagnato
wind	vento

How far is it?

... BY CAR/MOTORBIKE/BIKE

| **EXCUSE ME, HOW DO I GET TO ..., PLEASE?** | **SCUSI, PER ANDARE A ...?** |

How far is it?	Quanti chilometri sono?
Excuse me, is this the road to ...?	Scusi, è questa la strada per ...?
How do I get to the ... motorway?	Scusi, l'autostrada per ...?
Straight on until you get to ...	Sempre diritto fino a ...

Then ...
    at the traffic lights ...
    at the next corner ...
turn left/right.
	Poi ...
	    al semaforo ...
	    al prossimo angolo ...
	svolti a sinistra/destra.

| **FILL HER UP, PLEASE.** | **IL PIENO, PER FAVORE.** |

Where's the nearest petrol station, please?	Dov'è la prossima stazione di servizio, per favore?

...litres of ...
    three-star,
    four-star,
    diesel,
    unleaded/leaded.
	Vorrei ... litri di ...
	    benzina normale.
	    super.
	    gasolio.
	    senza piombo(verde)/con piombo.

Please check ...
    the oil.
    the tyre pressure.
	Per favore, controlli ...
	    il livello dell'olio.
	    la pressione delle gomme.

Please check the water, too.	Controlli anche l'acqua del radiatore, per favore.

17

PARKING — IL PARCHEGGIO

Is there a car-park near here?	Scusi, c'è un parcheggio qui vicino?
Can I park my car here?	Posso lasciare la macchina qui?

MY CAR'S BROKEN DOWN — HO UN GUASTO

I've got a flat tyre.	Ho una gomma a terra.
Would you send me ... ... a mechanic, ... a breakdown truck, please?	Mi potrebbe mandare ... ... un meccanico? ... un carro-attrezzi?
Could you lend me some petrol, please?	Mi potrebbe dare un po' di benzina, per favore?
Could you help me change the wheel, please?	Mi potrebbe aiutare a cambiare la ruota?
Could you give me a lift to the nearest petrol station?	Mi potrebbe dare un passaggio fino alla prossima stazione di servizio?
Can you give me a tow to the nearest garage?	Mi potrebbe rimorchiare fino alla prossima officina?

IS THERE A GARAGE NEAR HERE? — SCUSI SIGNORE/SIGNORA/SIGNORINA, C'È UN'OFFICINA QUI VICINO?

The car won't start.	La macchina non parte.
The battery is flat	La batteria è scarica.
There's something wrong with the engine.	Il motore non va bene.
The brakes don't work.	I freni non sono a posto.
... is/are faulty.	... è/sono difettoso/difettosi.
I'm losing oil.	La macchina perde olio.
Could you have a look?	Ci potrebbe dare un'occhiata, per favore?
Change the spark-plugs, please.	Cambi le candele, per favore.
How much will it be?	Quanto costerà?

THERE'S BEEN AN ACCIDENT | C'È STATO UN INCIDENTE

Please call ...	Chiami subito ...
an ambulance.	un'autoambulanza.
the police.	la polizia.
the fire-brigade.	i vigili del fuoco.

Have you got a first-aid kit?	Ha materiale di pronto soccorso?

It was my fault.	È stata colpa mia.

It was your fault.	È stata colpa Sua.

Shall we call the police, or can we settle things ourselves?	Dobbiamo chiamare la polizia, o ci vogliamo mettere d'accordo fra noi?

I'd like my insurance company to take care of the damage.	Vorrei far regolare il danno dalla mia assicurazione.

Please give me ...	Mi dia ...
... your name and address.	... il Suo nome e indirizzo.
... particulars of your insurance.	... nome e indirizzo della Sua Assicurazione.

Thank you very much for your help.	Grazie dell'aiuto.

CAR/MOTORBIKE/ BICYCLE HIRE | AUTONOLEGGIO/ NOLEGIO DI MOTOCICLI

I'd like to hire ...	Vorrei noleggiare per ... giorni/una settimana ...
a jeep.	un fuoristrada.
a car.	una macchina.
a motorbike/moped.	una moto/un motorino.
a scooter.	una motoretta.
a bike/tandem.	una bicicletta/un tandem.
for ... days/for a week.	

What do you charge per km?	Quanto si paga per ogni chilometro percorso?

Does the vehicle have comprehensive insurance?	Il veicolo è assicurato contro tutti i rischi?

Is it possible to leave the car in ...?	È possibile riconsegnare la macchina a ...?

On the road

Attenzione	(warning)
Bambini	(school children)
Cambio corsia	(change lanes)
Curva pericolosa	(dangerous bend)
Dare la precedenza	(give way)
Deviazione	(diversion)
Discesa pericolosa	(steep gradient)
Disco orario	(parking disc)
Divieto di inversione	(no U-turn)
Divieto di sorpasso	(no overtaking)
Divieto di sosta	(no parking/stopping)
Divieto di svolta a destra	(no right turn)
Dogana	(customs)
Galleria	(tunnel)
Incrocio	(crossroads)
Ingorgo	(traffic jam)
Lavori in corso	(roadworks)
Limitazione al peso	(weight limit)
Limite di velocità	(speed limit)
Mettersi in fila	(get in lane)
Ospedale	(hospital)
Parcheggio	(parking)
Passaggio pedonale	(zebra crossing)
Pericolo	(danger)
Pista ciclabile	(cycle path)
Ponte	(bridge)
Principiante	(learner)
Rallentare	(slow down)
Scontro, collisione	(collision)
Scuola	(school)
Semaforo	(traffic lights)
Senso unico	(one way)
Strada sdrucciolevole	(danger of skidding)
Strettoia	(road narrows)
Tenere la destra	(keep right)
Tenere libero l'accesso	(keep exit clear)
Uscita	(exit)
Vicolo cieco	(dead end)
Vietato al traffico	(no vehicles)
Vietato l'accesso	(no entry)
Zona a disco orario	(short-term parking [with parking disc])
Zona pedonale	(pedestrian zone)

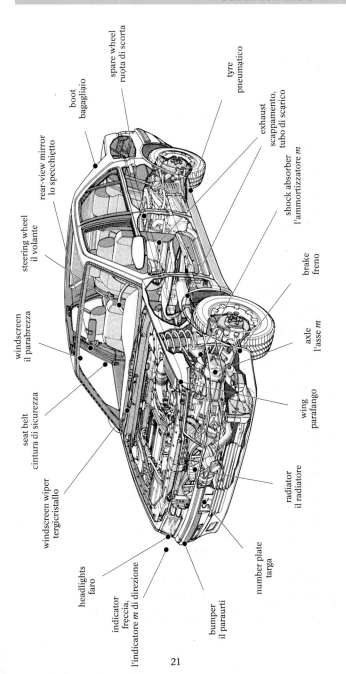

spare wheel
ruota di scorta

boot
bagagliaio

tyre
pneumatico

rear-view mirror
lo specchietto

exhaust
scappamento,
tubo di scarico

shock absorber
l'ammortizzatore *m*

steering wheel
il volante

brake
freno

windscreen
il parabrezza

axle
l'asse *m*

wing
parafango

seat belt
cintura di sicurezza

radiator
il radiatore

windscreen wiper
tergicristallo

headlights
faro

number plate
targa

indicator
freccia,
l'indicatore *m* di direzione

bumper
il paraurti

21

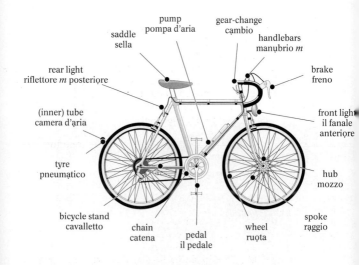

saddle
sella

pump
pompa d'aria

gear-change
cambio

handlebars
manubrio *m*

brake
freno

rear light
riflettore *m* posteriore

(inner) tube
camera d'aria

front light
il fanale
anteriore

tyre
pneumatico

hub
mozzo

bicycle stand
cavalletto

chain
catena

pedal
il pedale

wheel
ruota

spoke
raggio

accelerator	l'acceleratore *m*
alcohol level	per mille
automatic (transmission)	cambio automatico
backfire	l'accensione *f* a vuoto
bell	campanello
bend	curva
bicycle, bike	bicicletta
bonnet	cofano
box-spanner	la chiave fissa a tubo
brake lining	la guarnizione dei freni
breakdown	guasto
breakdown service	soccorso stradale
breakdown vehicle	carro attrezzi
cable	cavo
car body	carrozzeria
car park	parcheggio
car wash	autolavaggio
carburettor	il carburatore
carrier	il portabagagli
clutch	la frizione
cooling water	acqua di raffreddamento
country road	strada maestra
crash helmet	casco
crossroads, junction	incrocio
dipped headlights	le luci anabbaglianti
diversion	la deviazione
driving-licence	la patente

dynamo	la dinamo
emergency telephone	telefono d'emergenza
fan belt	cinghia
fault	difetto
fillingstation	stazione di servizio
fine	ammenda, multa
flat	gomma a terra
footbrake	freno a pedale
full-beam	i fari abbaglianti
fully comprehensive insurance	l'assicurazione *f* di totale copertura
fuse	sicurezza
garage	officina
gear lever	leva del cambio
gear	marcia
gearbox	cambio
gears	cambio
green card	carta verde
handbrake	freno a mano
hazard warning light	il lampeggiatore d'emergenza
heating	riscaldamento
hitch-hiker	l'autostoppista *m f*
horn	il clacson
hp (horsepower)	CV (cavalli vapore)
ignition key	chiavetta di accensione
ignition	l'accensione *f*
ignition switch	l'interruttore *m* dell'accensione
jack	il cric
jump lead	cavo ausiliario di collegamento per la messa in moto
lane	corsia
leathers	tuta impermeabile
lorry	il camion
motor, engine	il motore
motorbike	motocicletta
motorway	autostrada
mudguard	lamiera di protezione
multi-storey car park	parcheggio a più piani, autosilo
octane number	numero di ottani
oil change	cambio dell'olio
oil	olio
papers	i documenti
petrol	benzina
petrol can	lattina, tanica
petrol pump	pompa della benzina
(puncture) repair kit	gli accessori per la riparazione di forature
radar speed check	controllo radar
rim	il cerchione

road map	carta automobilistica
road	strada, via
roadworks	il cantiere edile
scooter	il motoscooter, motoretta
screw	la vite
sealing	la guarnizione
services	la stazione di servizio, posto di ristoro
short-circuit	corto circuito
sidelights	le luci di posizione
sign	il segnavia
spanner, wrench	la chiave per dadi
spark-plug	candela
speedometer	tachimetro
starter	motorino d'avviamento
street	strada, via
sunroof	tetto apribile
to tow away	rimorchiare, trainare
to turn (left/right)	svoltare
tools	l'utensile *m*, attrezzo
towrope	cavo da rimorchio
traffic jam	ingorgo
traffic lights	semaforo
valve	valvola
warning triangle	triangolo
wheel brace	la chiave a crociera

... BY PLANE

TAKE-OFF	DECOLLO
Where's the ... check-in counter?	Dov'è lo sportello della compagnia aerea ...?
When's the next flight to ...?	Quando c'è un aereo per ...?
I'd like to book a single/ return flight to ...	Vorrei prenotare un volo di sola an-data/di andata e ritorno per ...
Are there still seats available?	Ci sono ancora posti liberi?
Non-smoking, please.	Non fumatori, per favore.
I'd like to cancel this flight.	Vorrei annullare questo volo.
I'd like to change the booking.	Vorrei prendere un altro volo.
When do I have to be at the airport?	A che ora devo essere all'aeroporto?

Can I take this as hand luggage?	Posso portare appresso il bagaglio a mano?
Is the plane to ... late?	L'aereo per ... è in ritardo?

ARRIVAL	**ARRIVO**
My luggage is missing.	Il mio bagaglio è stato smarrito.
My suitcase has been damaged.	La mia valigia è stata danneggiata.

airline	compagnia aerea
airport tax	i diritti aeroportuali
boarding card	carta d'imbarco
booking	la prenotazione
to cancel	annullare
captain	capitano
to change the booking	cambiare il biglietto
connection	coincidenza
counter	sportello
delay	ritardo
direct flight	volo diretto
duty-free shop	spaccio porto-franco / duty free
emergency chute	scivolo d'emergenza
emergency exit	uscita d'emergenza
emergency landing	atterraggio di fortuna
to fasten one's seat belt	allacciare le cinture
flight	volo
hand luggage/baggage	bagaglio a mano
landing	atterraggio
life-jacket	giubbetto di salvataggio
luggage	bagaglio
non-smoker	non fumatore
on board	a bordo
passenger	passeggero
pilot	il/la pilota
plane	aereo
route	tratto (di volo)
scheduled time of departure	volo regolare
seat belt	cintura di sicurezza
security control	controllo di sicurezza
smoker	fumatore
steward/stewardess	lo steward, l'assistente m f di bordo/ l'hostess f
time of arrival	orario d'arrivo
window seat	posto al finestrino

... BY TRAIN

DEPARTURE	PARTENZA
When's the next train to ...?	Quando parte il prossimo treno per ...
A second-class/first-class single to ..., please.	Un biglietto di andata, seconda/prima classe per ...
Two returns to ..., please.	Due biglietti per ..., andata e ritorno, per favore.
Is there a reduction for children/students?	C'è una riduzione per bambini/per studenti?
I'd like to reserve a seat on the ... o'clock train to ...	Vorrei prenotare un posto per il treno delle ... per ..., per favore.
I'd like to register this case.	Vorrei spedire questa valigia come bagaglio appresso.
Where shall I put my bicycle during the journey?	Dove posso consegnare la mia bicicletta per la spedizione?
Is the train from ... running late?	È in ritardo il treno proveniente da ...?
Is there a connection to .../a ferry at ...?	A ... c'è la coincidenza per .../con il traghetto?
(Where) Do I have to change?	(Dove) Devo cambiare?
Which platform does the ... train leave from?	Da quale binario parte il treno per ...?

ON THE TRAIN	IN TRENO
Excuse me, is this seat free?	Scusi, è libero questo posto?
Does this train stop in ...?	Questo treno si ferma a ...?

Information signs

Acqua non potabile	*(not drinking water)*
Freno d'emergenza	*(emergency brake/communication cord)*
Fumatori	*(smoking [compartment])*
Non Fumatori	*(non-smoking [compartment])*
Libero	*(free/unoccupied)*
Occupato	*(occupied)*
Ritirata	*(toilets)*

to arrive	arrivare
compartment	scompartimento
departure	partenza
emergency brake	freno d'emergenza
fare	prezzo del biglietto
fast train	direttissimo
to get on	salire
to get out	scendere
half fare (child)	biglietto per ragazzi
left-luggage office	deposito bagagli
left-luggage ticket	lo scontrino bagagli
local train	diretto
luggage	bagaglio
main station	la stazione centrale
motorail service	treno traghetto
no-smoking compartment	scompartimento per non fumatori
platform	binario
railway	ferrovia
reduction	la riduzione
reservation	la prenotazione
restaurant car	il vagone ristorante
return ticket	biglietto di andata e ritorno
seat reservation	biglietto di prenotazione posto
smoking compartment	scompartimento per fumatori
station	la stazione
stop	fermata
supplement	supplemento
ticket	biglietto
ticket office	biglietteria
time of departure	orario di partenza
timetable	orario
toilet	gabinetto
train-ferry	la nave traghetto
waiting-room	sala d'aspetto

... BY BOAT

AT THE PORT | **AL PORTO**

Where does ...	Da dove parte ...
When does ...	Quando parte ...
the next ship/the next ferry	la prossima nave/ il prossimo traghetto
leave for ...?	per ...?
I'd like a ticket to ...	Vorrei un biglietto per ...

Where's the restaurant/lounge?	Dov'è il ristorante/il salone?
I don't feel well.	Non mi sento bene.
Could you give me something for sea-sickness, please.	Mi dia qualcosa contro il mal di mare, per favore.

booking	la prenotazione
cabin	cabina
to call at	toccare, fare scalo
captain	capitano
carferry	autotraghetto
coast	costa
cruise	crociera
deck	coperta
dock	approdo
excursion	l'escursione *f* a terra
ferry	traghetto
hovercraft	l'hovercraft *m*
jetfoil, hydrofoil	aliscafo
landing-stage	il pontile d'approdo
lifebelt	il salvagente
lifeboat	scialuppa di salvataggio
life-jacket	giubbetto di salvataggio
mainland, dry land	terraferma
motorboat	motoscafo
on board	a bordo
passenger	passeggero
port	babordo
port	porto
rough seas	moto ondoso
rowing-boat	barca a remi
to sail	uscire dal porto, salpare
sailing-boat	barca a vela
to be seasick	avere il mal di mare
starboard	tribordo
steamer, steamship	piroscafo, nave a vapore
steward	il cameriere
ticket	biglietto
tour	giro
trainferry	la nave traghetto
wave	il surf, onda
yacht	panfilo

What to see and where to go

I'd like a map of the town, please.	Vorrei una pianta della città.
What places of interest are there here?	Che cosa c'è da vedere qui?
Are there sightseeing tours of the city?	Ci sono giri turistici della città organizzati?
How much does the tour cost?	Quanto costa il biglietto?
Are we going to see ..., too?	Si va anche a vedere ...?
When are we going back?	Quando si parte per il viaggio di ritorno?

SIGHTS

When's the museum open?	Quando è aperto il museo?
When does the tour start?	Quando comincia la visita con la guida?
Is this (that) ...?	È questo il .../È questa la ...?

altar	l'altare *m*
architecture	architettura
building	edificio
castle	castello
castle	fortezza
cathedral	duomo, la cattedrale
cemetery	cimitero
century	secolo

In the history of art and literature, the centuries (from the 13th century onwards) are referred to as follows:
il Duecento (the 13th century – literally *"the two hundred"),*
il Trecento (the 14th century – *"the three hundred")* and so on up to
il Novecento (the 20th century).

chapel	cappella
church	chiesa
city centre	centro
countryside	paesaggio
day trip	gita di un giorno
drawing	disegno
emperor/empress	imperatore/imperatrice
excavations	gli scavi
excursion, trip	gita
exhibition	mostra, l'esposizione *f*
forest	bosco
fortress, castle	fortezza
gallery	galleria (d'arte)
guide	guida turistica, il cicerone
guided tour	visita guidata
king	re
lake	lago
market	mercato
covered market	mercato coperto
monument	monumento
mountain(s)	montagna
museum	museo
nature reserve	parco nazionale
painter	pittore/pittrice
painting	dipinto
painting	pittura
palace	palazzo
picture	quadro
queen	regina
religion	la religione
restoration	restauro
ruin	rovina
scenery	paesaggio
sculptor	lo scultore
sculpture	scultura
sights	le cose da vedersi, attrazioni
sightseeing tour of the town/city	giro della città
square	piazza
the old town	centro storico
service	messa, la funzione sacra
tour	giro
tour	visita
tower	la torre
town hall	municipio
vantage point	il belvedere
zoo	lo zoo

What's on the menu?

EATING OUT

Is there ... here?
  a good restaurant
  a restaurant with local specialities
	Scusi, mi potrebbe indicare ...
	  un buon ristorante?
	  un locale tipico?

Would you reserve us a table for four for this evening, please?	Può riservarci per stasera un tavolo per quattro persone?
Is this table/seat free?	È libero questo tavolo/questo posto?
A table for two/three, please.	Per favore, un tavolo per due/tre persone.
Where are the toilets, please?	Mi può dire dov'è la toilette, per favore?
Cheers!	Alla Sua salute! / Salute!
Do you mind if I smoke?	Posso fumare?

ORDERING / L'ORDINAZIONE

Waiter, could I have ..., please.
  the menu
  drinks list
  the winelist
	Cameriere, ..., per favore.
	  il menu
	  la lista delle bevande
	  la lista dei vini

What can you recommend?	Che cosa mi consiglia?

What would you like ...
  as a starter?
  for your main course?
  for dessert?
	Che cosa prende ...
	  per antipasto?
	  per secondo piatto?
	  per dessert?

I'll have ...	Prendo ...
I'm afraid we've run out of ...	Purtroppo il/la... è finito.

31

How would you like your meat?	Come vuole la carne?
well-done	ben cotta
medium	non troppo cotta
rare	al sangue
What would you like to drink?	Che cosa desidera da bere?
A glass of ..., please.	Per favore, un bicchiere di ...
A bottle of ..., please.	Per favore, una bottiglia di ...
Bring us ..., please.	Ci porti, per favore ...

COMPLAINTS — RECLAMI

Have you forgotten my ...?	Ha dimenticato il mio/la mia ...?
I didn't order that.	Non ho ordinato questo.
Fetch the manager, please.	Mi chiami per favore il direttore/il proprietario!

Where to eat

osteria – A type of wine bar which mostly serves local wines and sometimes dishes of regional food are available.

trattoria – This is usually a family-run establishment where you can get classic Italian home-cooking.

ristorante – You will find a detailed menu displayed outside most Italian restaurants, but remember that if you go to a restaurant in Italy you will be expected to eat a large three course meal. This consists of a soup, rice or pasta dish for the first course, followed by fish or meat for the second and fruit or dessert to finish off. If you only want a plate of spaghetti or just a quick bite to eat you should go to a ...

tavola calda – Here you can get a variety of hot snacks which you can even eat standing up.

bar – Café where Italians go at any time of day to drink their *espresso, macchiato, cappuccino* or aperitif and eat little snacks either standing at the bar or sitting at a table. Before you make your order at the bar, you have to go to the till and get a *scontrino* (ticket). It's advisable to have some small change ready. The price list *(listino prezzi)* displayed only refers to items which are consumed at the bar. It costs more if you want to sit down.

paninoteca – A sandwich bar where you can get hot or cold filled rolls. Paninotecas are mostly frequented by young people.

COULD I HAVE THE BILL, PLEASE?	**IL CONTO, PER FAVORE**

All together, please.	Tutto insieme.
Separate bills, please.	Conti separati, per favore.
Did you enjoy your meal?	Era di Suo gradimento?
The food was excellent.	Il mangiare era eccellente.
That's for you.	Questo è per Lei.
Keep the change.	Il resto è per Lei.

"Acqua in bocca!"

You use this expression, which literally means *"water in the mouth"*, if you want someone to keep a secret. It's similar to the English expression *"keep it under your hat"*.

---

baked	al forno
to boil	bollire
breakfast	prima colazione → p.35
children's portion	la mezza porzione
cold	freddo
cook *(noun)*	cuoco/cuoca
to cook	cuocere
cup	tazza
cutlery	le posate
dessert, sweet	il dessert, il dolce → p.40
diabetic	diabetico
dinner	cena
dish of the day	piatto del giorno
dish	pietanza
drink	bevanda → p.41
fishbone	spina, lisca
fork	forchetta
fresh	fresco
fried	fritto
garlic	aglio
glass	il bicchiere
home-made	fatto in casa
hors d'œuvre, starter	antipasto → p.36

Service included?

The prices listed on any menu usually include a cover charge (*coperto*). This charge is always payable regardless of the size of your order. The bread and *grissini* which are laid on every table, however, are free.

hot	caldo, bollente
hot *(spicy)*	piccante
knife	coltello
lemon	il limone
lunch	pranzo
main course	secondo → p.37
menu	il menù
mustard	la senape
oil	olio
order	l'ordinazione *f*
pepper	il pepe
plate	piatto
portion	la porzione
raw	crudo
roasted	arrostito
salt	il sale
sauce	salsa
saucer	piattino
to season	condire, drogare
seasoning, spice	le spezie
serviette, napkin	tovagliolo
set meal/menu	menù
side-dish	contorno
smoked	affumicato
soup	minestra, zuppa → p.36
sour	agro
speciality	specialità
spoon	cucchiaio
straw	cannuccia
sugar	zucchero
sweet	dolce
sweetener	saccarina, dolcificante
tender	tenero
tip	mancia
toothpick	lo stuzzicadenti
tough	duro
vegetarian	vegetariano
vinegar	aceto
waiter	cameriere
waiter/waitress	il cameriere/la cameriera
water	acqua
well-done	ben cotto

Mopping up

It is customary when you have finished what's on your plate to
"Fare la scarpetta" which means *"to mop up the sauce with your bread"*.

34

Carte
Menu

Prima colazione	Breakfast
caffè	black coffee
caffellatte	white coffee
caffè decaffeinizzato	decaffeinated coffee
tè al latte/al limone	tea with milk/lemon
una tisana	herbal tea
cioccolata	hot chocolate
una spremuta	fruit juice
un uovo à la coque	boiled egg
uova strapazzate	scrambled egg
uova con lo speck	egg and bacon
pane/panini/pane tostato	bread/rolls/toast
un cornetto	croissant
burro	butter
formaggio	cheese
salume	cooked or smoked sausage
prosciutto	cured ham
miele	honey
marmellata	jam
pappa di fiocchi d'avena e frutta	muesli
uno iogurt	Yoghurt
della frutta	fresh fruit → p. 40

Caffè ≠ coffee

In Italy when you order a *caffé* you will always get an espresso unless you specify otherwise. There are many different types of espresso. *Caffé ristretto*, for instance, is stronger than a normal espresso. *Caffé lungo* is diluted with water. *Caffé macchiato* is served with a dash of milk. *Caffé corretto* is espresso with grappa and is usually drunk after a meal as an aid to digestion. Italians never drink cappuccino after a meal or in the afternoon, but only for breakfast.

Antipasti	Appetisers
acciughe	anchovies
affettato misto	sliced pork meats (ham, salami, mortadella etc.)
anguilla affumicata	smoked eel
aragosta	lobster/crayfish
carciofini sott'olio	artichoke hearts in oil
funghi sott'olio	mushrooms in oil
gamberi	prawns
melone e prosciutto	melon and cured ham
prosciutto cotto	cooked ham
prosciutto crudo	cured ham
prosciutto con fichi freschi	Parma ham with fresh figs
tonno con fagioli	tuna fish with haricot beans

Minestre	Soups
minestra di riso	rice soup
minestra di verdura	vegetable soup
minestrone	thick vegetable soup
pasta e fagioli	pasta and bean soup
pastina in brodo	consommé with small pasta shapes
Stracciatella	Roman egg soup
zuppa di pesce	fish soup
zuppa pavese	soup topped with a slice of fried bread and an egg

Primi Piatti	Starters
spaghetti	spaghetti
–al burro/in bianco	with butter
–alla napoletana/ al pomodoro	with tomato sauce (without meat)
–alla bolognese/al ragù	with bolognese sauce
–alle vongole	with clams
–alla carbonara	with eggs and bacon
–alla panna	with cream
–aglio olio	with oil
–alla puttanesca	with tomato sauce, olives and hot spices

Spoilt for choice

There is no shortage of choice when it comes to starters in Italy which are generally very abundant. The main dish is usually either a piece of meat or fish which comes unaccompanied, so if you want a side-dish (*contorno*) of vegetables to go with it, you will need to order it separately.

gnocchi alla romana	semolina gnocchi baked with butter and cheese
polenta (alla valdostana)	cornmeal (with melted cheese)
agnolotti/ravioli/tortellini	stuffed pasta parcels
cannelloni	pasta rolls, stuffed and baked
fettuccine/tagliatelle	pasta strips
lasagne al forno	baked lasagne
lasagne verdi	spinach lasagne
maccheroni	macaroni
vermicelli	thin spaghetti
risotto alla milanese	risotto with saffron
risotto con funghi	risotto with mushrooms

Carni	Meat
abbacchio	baby lamb
agnello	lamb
anitra	duck
arrosto di vitello	roast veal
bistecca ai ferri	grilled steak
bollito misto	a selection of boiled meats
capretto	baby goat
cervello	brain
coniglio	rabbit
cotoletta alla milanese	sautéed breaded veal escalopes
cotoletta di maiale	pork chops
fegato	liver
fesa di vitello	veal chops
lepre	hare
lingua	tongue
maiale	pork
lombata di vitello	loin of veal
manzo/bue	beef
montone	mutton
oca	goose
ossobuco	knuckle of veal
petti di pollo	breast of chicken
piccione	pigeon
pollo	chicken
pollo arrosto	roast chicken
polpette (svizzere)	meatballs
rognoni	kidneys
saltimbocca alla romana	veal escalopes with prosciutto and sage
scaloppine di vitello	small escalopes of veal
spezzatino	stew with tomatoes
stufato	pot-roast
tacchino	turkey
trippa	tripe
vitello	veal
zampone	stuffed pig's trotter

If you want a pizza for dinner, you will need to find a *"pizzeria"*, as pizzas are **not** usually offered on restaurant menus.

Pesce	Fish
anguilla	eel
aragosta	crayfish/lobster
calamari	squid
cozze/vongole	mussels/clams
datteri di mare	date mussels
fritto di pesce	fried fish
frutti di mare	seafood
gambero	prawns
granchio	crab
pesce spada	swordfish
rana pescatrice	monkfish
passera di mare	plaice
salmone	salmon
scampi fritti	scampi
sgombro	mackerel
sogliola	sole
triglia	mullet
tonno	tuna
trota	trout

Verdura e contorni	Vegetables
asparagi	asparagus
bietola	Swiss chard
broccoli	broccoli
carciofi	artichoke
carote	carrots
cavolfiore	cauliflower
cavolo	cabbage
cicoria	chicory

I couldn't give a cabbage!

There are many different colloquial expression which use the word *"cavolo"* (cabbage).
"non capisco un cavolo" (I can't understand a word)
"non so un cavolo" (I haven't the faintest idea)
"non me ne importa un cavolo" (I couldn't care less)
"non vale un cavolo" (it's not worth a fig)
"cavolo" can also express something negative. For instance
"un film del cavolo" means *"a lousy film"*.

fagioli	cannellini beans
fagiolini	French beans
finocchi	fennel
funghi	mushrooms
lenticchie	lentils
melanzane	aubergines
patate	potatoes
patatine fritte	French fries, chips
peperoni	peppers
piselli	peas
pomodori	tomatoes
purè di patate	mashed potato
ravanelli	radishes
sedano	celery
spinaci	spinach
zucchini	courgettes

Insalate	Salads
insalata mista	mixed salad
insalata russa	Russian salad
insalata verde	green salad
radicchio	radicchio (red-leafed chicory)

Uova	Eggs
frittata	omelette
uova al tegame	fried egg
uova sode	hard-boiled egg
uova strapazzate	scrambled egg

Formaggi	Cheese
bel paese	bel paese
gorgonzola	gorgonzola
gruviera	gruyère
mozzarella	mozzarella
parmigiano/grana	parmesan/grana
pecorino	a hard sheep's milk cheese
provolone (affumicato)	a smoked buffalo's milk cheese (now more commonly made with cow's milk)
ricotta	ricotta
stracchino	a soft mild cheese produced in Northern Italy
taleggio	a type of stracchino with red rind

Dolci e frutta	Fruit and desserts
budino	bread/plum pudding
crème caramel	caramel custard
cassata	ice cream with candied fruit
frutta cotta	stewed fruit
gelato	ice cream
macedonia	fruit salad
pasta	small pastry
tiramisù	tiramisu
torta	cake, tart
zabaione/zabaglione	dessert made of egg yolks, sugar and marsala
zuppa inglese	trifle
albicocca	apricot
ananas	pineapple
arancia	orange
ciliegie	cherries
cocomero/anguria	water melon
fichi	figs
fragole	strawberries
lamponi	raspberries
mela	apple
melone	melon
mirtilli rossi	cranberries
pera	pear
pesca	peach
pompelmo	grapefruit
prugna/susina	plum
uva	grapes

Gelati	Ice cream
albicocca	apricot
cioccolata	chocolate
coppa assortita	assorted flavours
coppa con panna	topped with whipped cream
fior di latte	cream
fragola	strawberry
lampone	raspberry
limone	lemon
mirtilli	blueberry
nocciola	hazelnut
tartufo	truffle
vaniglia/crema	vanilla

Lista delle bevande
Beverages

Vini	Wine
Aleatico	sweet red wine from Tuscany
Asti spumante	sparkling wine from Piedmont
Barbera	medium dry red wine from Piedmont
Bardolino	red table wine from the Lake Garda region
Chianti	a fairly full-bodied wine from Tuscany
Frascati	medium dry white wine from the "Castelli" region near Rome
Grignolino	dry red wine from Piedmont
Lacrima Christi	a fairly sweet, full-bodied red wine from the region around Naples
Lambrusco	a slightly sparkling red wine from the Modena-Bologna region
Marino	dry white wine from the "Castelli Romani"
Marsala	sweet, rich red wine from Sicily
Moscato	muscatel
Orvieto	a fine dry or sweet white wine
Ruffino	red wine from Tuscany
Valpolicella	red wine from Verona

Birre	Beer
birra scura/chiara	bitter/lager
birra al malto	stout
birra forte	strong beer
birra alla spina	draught beer

Bevande analcoliche — Non-alcoholic drinks

Bevande analcoliche	Non-alcoholic drinks
acqua minerale	mineral water
acqua di seltz	soda water
amarena	cherry juice
aranciata	orangeade
gassosa	fizzy, sparkling
spremuta di limone	freshly squeezed lemon juice (with sugar and water)
succo di frutta	fruit juice
succo di mele	apple juice
succo di pomodoro	tomato juice
succo d'uva	grape juice

Caffetteria — Hot drinks

Caffetteria	Hot drinks
caffè, espresso	small, strong coffee
caffè macchiato	small, strong coffee with a dash of milk
cappuccino	coffee with hot, frothy milk
camomilla	camomile tea
tè al latte/limone	tea with milk/lemon
tè alla menta	peppermint tea
tè alla frutta	fruit tea
cioccolata con panna	hot chocolate with cream

Liquori — Brandies and liqueurs

Liquori	Brandies and liqueurs
amaro	bitters
grappa	a spirit distilled from fermented remains of grapes after pressing
sambuca	aniseed liqueur
Vecchia Romagna	Italian cognac

Do you accept credit cards?

open...... aperto	closed............. chiuso	
closed for holidays....... chiuso per ferie		

Where can I find ...?	Dove si può trovare ...?
Can you recommend a ... shop?	Mi può indicare un negozio di ...?
I'd like ...	Vorrei ...
Have you got ...?	Ha ...?
I'll take it.	Lo prendo.
How much is it?	Quanto costa?
Do you take ... eurocheques? credit cards?	Accetta ... eurocheques? carte di credito?

antique shop	negozio di antichità
arts and crafts	artigianato artistico, arti decorative
baker	panificio
bookshop	libreria → p. 54
butcher	macelleria
cake shop	pasticceria
chemist (including pre-scriptions)	farmacia → p. 44
chemist/drugstore	profumeria → p. 46
delicatessen	negozio di specialità gastronomiche
department store	il grande magazzino
dry-cleaner	lavanderia a secco, tintoria
electrical goods	l'elettricista m → p. 47
fishmonger	pescheria
flea market	mercato delle pulci
florist	fioraio
food store	(negozio di generi) alimentari → p. 49
fruiterer	fruttivendolo
greengrocer	erbivendolo

hairdresser	il parrucchiere → p. 50
health food shop	negozio di prodotti dietetici
household goods	negozio di casalinghi → p. 51
jeweller	gioielleria → p. 52
launderette	lavanderia a gettone
laundry	lavanderia
leather shop	pelletteria
market	mercato
music shop	negozio di articoli musicali
newsagent	giornalaio → p. 54
off-licence	rivendita di prodotti alcolici, bottiglieria
optician	ottico → p. 52
perfumery	profumeria
photographic materials	gli articoli fotografici → p. 53
second-hand bookshop	antiquariato
self-service shop	il self-service
shoe shop	negozio di calzature → p. 53
souvenir shop	i souvenirs
sports shop	gli articoli sportivi
stationer	cartoleria → p. 54
supermarket	supermercato
tobacconist's	tabaccaio → p. 54
toy shop	negozio di giocattoli
travel agency	agenzia viaggi
watchmaker	orologiaio
wine merchant	fiaschetteria

CHEMIST'S (FOR PRESCRIPTIONS)	FARMACIA
Where's the nearest chemist's (with all-night service)?	Dov'è la farmacia (di turno) più vicina?
Can you give me something for ...?	Mi dia qualcosa contro ..., per favore.
You need a prescription for this.	Ci vuole una ricetta per questa medicina.

to be taken internally	per uso interno
for external use only	per uso esterno, esteriore
to take	prendere
on an empty stomach	a stomaco vuoto
before meals	prima dei pasti
after meals	dopo i pasti
let it melt in your mouth	far sciogliere in bocca

antibiotics	antibiotico
antidote	antidoto
aspirin®	aspirina®
camomile tea	camomilla
cardiac stimulant	medicamento per disturbi circolatori
charcoal tablets	l'astringente *m* intestinale a base di caolino carbone
condom	preservativo, profilattico
contraceptive pills	le pillole anticoncezionali
cotton-wool	il cotone idrofilo
cough mixture	sciroppo (contro la tosse)
disinfectant	il disinfettante
drops	le gocce
ear-drops	le gocce per gli orecchi
elastic bandage	benda elastica
eye drops	le gocce per gli occhi, collirio
gargle	la soluzione per gargarismi
gauze bandage	fascia di garza
glucose	glucosio
headache tablets	le compresse contro il mal di testa
indigestion drops	digestivo in gocce
insect repellent	l'insetticida *m*
insulin	insulina
laxative	lassativo
medicine	medicina, farmaco
ointment for burns	pomata per le scottature
ointment	pomata
pain-killing tablets	le compresse contro il dolore, gli analgesici
plaster	cerotto
powder	cipria, borotalco
prescription	ricetta
remedy, medicine	medicina
sedative, tranquilizer	il calmante
side effects	le reazioni secondarie
sleeping pills	i sonniferi
sunburn	scottatura (solare)
suppository	supposta
tablet, pill	compressa
thermometer	termometro
throat lozenges	le pastiglie per la gola
(tincture of) iodine	tintura di iodio

CHEMIST'S (FOR TOILETRIES) — PROFUMERIA

after-shave lotion	la lozione dopobarba
body lotion	il latte per il corpo
brush	spazzola
cleansing milk	il latte detergente
comb	il pettine
condom	preservativo
cotton-wool	il cotone idrofilo
cream	crema
deodorant	il deodorante
detergent	detersivo
dummy	ciuccio, succhietto
eye-shadow	ombretto
feeding bottle	il biberon
flannel	guanto di spugna, manopola
hairbrush	spazzola per i capelli
lipstick	rossetto
manicure set	il necessaire da viaggio
mascara	il mascara
mirror	specchio
nail-brush	spazzolino per le unghie
nail-file	limetta
nail-scissors	le forbici per le unghie
nail-varnish	smalto
nappies	i pannolini
paper handkerchiefs	i fazzoletti di carta
perfume, scent	profumo
plaster	cerotto
protection factor	il fattore protettivo
razor	rasoio (elettrico)
razor-blade	la lametta
rouge	il rouge
safety-pins	spilla da balia
sanitary towels	gli assorbenti
setting lotion	la frizione
shampoo	lo shampoo
shaving-brush	pennello da barba
shaving-soap	il sapone da barba
soap	il sapone
sponge	spugna
suntan lotion	crema solare
suntan oil	olio solare
tampons	i tamponi
toilet-paper	carta igienica
toothbrush	spazzolino da denti
toothpaste	dentifricio
tweezers	le pinzette

ELECTRICAL GOODS | L'ELETTRICISTA

adapter	l'adattatore *m*
battery	batteria
cassette	cassetta, il caricatore
CD, compact disc	il CD, il compact disc
hair-dryer	il föhn
headphones	cuffia
personal stereo	il walkman®
plug	spina
record	disco
torch	lampadina tascabile
video film	il videofilm
video camera	videocamera
video cassette	videocassetta
video recorder	il videoregistratore

FASHION | MODA

Can you show me ...?	Mi può mostrare ...?
Can I try it on?	Posso provarlo?
What size do you take?	Che taglia porta?

It's too ...
    tight/big
    short/long.
    small/big.
	Questo mi è troppo ...
	    stretto/largo.
	    corto/lungo.
	    piccolo/grande.

It's a good fit. I'll take it.	Va bene. Lo prendo.
It's not quite what I wanted.	Non è proprio quello che volevo.
I'd like to have these things cleaned/washed.	Vorrei far lavare a secco/lavare questa roba.
When will they be ready?	Quando sarà pronta?

anorak	giacca a vento
bathing trunks	il costume da bagno
bikini	il bikini
blouse	camicetta
cap	berretto
cardigan	giacca di lana, il golf
coat	cappotto, soprabito
colour	tinta, il colore
dress	vestito
dressing-gown (robe)	vestaglia

Conversion of Italian sizes

Ladies' suits and dresses

Italy	40	42	44	46	48
UK	8	10	12	14	16
USA	6	8	10	12	14

Men's suits and coats

Italy	46	48	50	52	54
UK/USA	36	38	40	42	44

Shoes

Italy	38	39	40	41	42	43	44	45	46
UK	5	6	6½	7	7½	8½	9½	10½	11
USA	6½	7½	8	8½	9	9½	10½	11½	12

gloves	i guanti
handbag	borsa
handkerchief	fazzoletto
hat	cappello
jacket	giacca
jumper	il golf
lining	fodera
nightdress	camicia da notte
panties	lo slip
pants (*underwear*)	le mutande
pants (*US*)	i pantaloni, i calzoni
pullover, jumper	il pullover, il maglione
pyjamas	il pigiama
raincoat	l'impermeabile *m*
scarf	lo scialle; sciarpa
shirt	camicia
skirt	gonna
socks	i calzini
(sports)jacket	giacca
stockings	le calze
striped	a righe
suit (*men's*)	abito
suit (*women's*)	il tailleur
summer dress	vestito estivo
swimming costume	il costume da bagno
tie	cravatta
tights	il collant, calzamaglia
tracksuit	tuta da ginnastica
umbrella	ombrello
vest	maglietta, canottiera
waistcoat	il gilè

cotton	il cotone	linen	lino
(terry) towelling	spugna	silk	seta
synthetic fibre	fibra sintetica	wool	lana

FOOD AND DRINK	ALIMENTARI

You will find a more comprehensive vocabulary list in the FOOD & DRINK section on p. 35.

What can I get you?	Cosa desịdera?
I'd like ..., please.	Mi dịa ..., per favore.
one kilo of ...	un chilo di ...
100 grams of ...	un etto di ...
a piece of ...	un pezzo di ...
a packet of ...	un pacco di ...
a jar of ...	un bicchịere di ...
a tin of ...	una scạtola di ...
a bottle of ...	una bottịglia di ...
a bag, please.	un sacchetto/una sportina.
Can I get you anything else?	Altro?
No, thank you. That's all.	Nient'altro, grạzie.

baby food	alimenti per la prima infanzia → p. 67
beer	birra
alcohol-free beer	birra analcọlica
biscuits	i biscotti → p. 40
bread	il pane
a loaf of bread	una pagnotta
butter	burro
cake	torta, il dolce
cheese	formạggio → p. 39
chicken	pollo
chocolate	cioccolata
coffee	il caffè → p. 35, 42
cream	panna
eggs	le uọva
fish	il pesce → p. 38
flour	farina
fresh	fresco
fruit	frutta → p. 40
ice-cream	gelato → p. 40
jam	marmellata → p. 35
lemonade	limonata
margarine	margarina
meat	la carne → p. 37
milk	il latte
low-fat milk	il latte magro
mince, minced meat	la carne tritata
mineral water	acqua minerale

nuts	le noci
oil	olio
orange juice	succo d'arancia
pasta	pasta
roll	panino → p. 35
salad	insalata → p. 39
salt	il sale
sausages	le salsicce
soup	minestra → p. 36
sweets	i dolciumi → p. 40
tea	il tè → p. 35, 42
tea bag	bustina di tè
toast	il toast
vegetables	verdura → p. 38
wine	vino → p. 41
yoghurt	lo iogurt

HAIRDRESSER'S — IL PARRUCCHIERE

Can I make an appointment for tomorrow?	Posso prendere un appuntamento per domani?
Shampoo ... and blow dry, and set, please.	Shampoo ... e föhn, e messa in piega, per favore.
Wash and cut/Dry cut, please.	Tagliare e/senza lavare, per favore.
I'd like ... a perm. to have my hair dyed/tinted. to have my hair highlighted/lowlighted. to have my hair streaked.	Vorrei ... una permanente. farmi tingere i capelli. un riflessante. farmi le mèche.
Not too short/Very short/A bit shorter, please.	Non troppo corti/Molto corti/Un po' più corti, per favore.
I'd like a shave, please.	La barba, per favore.
Would you trim my beard, please?	Mi spunti la barba, per favore.
Thank you. That's fine.	Grazie. Va bene così.

beard	barba
blond(e)	biondo
to blow dry	asciugare con il föhn
to comb	pettinare

curlers	i bigodini
curls	i ricci
dandruff	forfora
to do someone's hair	pettinare
to dye	tingere
fringe	frangetta
hair	i capelli
haircut	taglio
hairpiece	il toupet
hairspray	lacca
hairstyle	pettinatura
moustache	i baffi
parting	riga
perm	la permanente
to set	mettere in piega
shampoo	lo shampoo
to have a shave	farsi fare la barba
to tint	tingere
wig	parrucca

HOUSEHOLD GOODS — ARTICOLI CASALINGHI

bin liner	sacco delle immondizie
bottle-opener	l'apribottiglie *m*
broom	scopa
bucket	secchio
candles	le candele
charcoal	carbonella
cling foil	pellicola (per la conservazione dei cibi)
cold bag	borsa frigo
corkscrew	il cavatappi
firelighters	il combustibile solido
glass	il bicchiere
grill	griglia
ice pack	piastra refrigerante
knife, fork and spoon	le posate
methylated spirits	spirito industriale
paper napkins	i tovagliolini di carta
paraffin	petrolio
pocket knife	temperino, coltello tascabile
sunshade	l'ombrellone *m*
tin foil	foglio di alluminio
tin-opener	l'apriscatole *m*

JEWELLER'S — DAL GIOIELLIERE

My watch doesn't work. Could you have a look at it?	Il mio orologio non va più. Potrebbe darci un'occhiata?
I'd like a nice souvenir/present.	Vorrei un bel ricordo/regalo.

bracelet	braccialetto
brooch	spilla
crystal	cristallo
earrings	gli orecchini
gold	oro
jewellery	gioielli
necklace	collana
pearl	perla
pendant	ciondolo
ring	anello
silver	argento
wristwatch	orologio da polso

OPTICIAN'S — OTTICO

Could you repair these glasses/frames for me, please?	Mi potrebbe aggiustare, questi occhiali/la montatura, per favore?
One of the lenses of my glasses is broken.	Mi si è rotta una lente degli occhiali.
I'm short-sighted/long-sighted.	Sono miope/presbite.
What's your acuity?	Che capacità visiva ha?
plus/minus ... in the right eye, ... in the left eye ...	destra più/meno ..., sinistra ...
When can I pick up the glasses?	Quando posso venire a prendere gli occhiali?
I need ... contact lens solution some cleansing solution for hard/soft contact lenses.	Ho bisogno di ... soluzione per la conservazione soluzione detergente per lenti a contatto rigide/morbide.
I'm looking for ... some sunglasses. some binoculars.	Vorrei ... un paio di occhiali da sole. un binocolo.

PHOTOGRAPHIC MATERIALS | GLI ARTICOLI FOTOGRAFICI

I'd like ...	Vorrei ...
I'd like ...	Vorrei ...
a film for this camera.	una pellicola per questa macchina.
a colour film (for slides)	una pellicola a colori (per dia-positive).
a film with 36/20/12 ex-posures.	una pellicola da 36/20/12.

Could you put the film in the camera for me, please?

Mi può inserire la pellicola, per favore?

When can I pick up the photos?

Quando posso venire a prendere le foto?

The view-finder/shutter doesn't work.

Il mirino/Lo scatto non funziona.

This doesn't work. Can you mend it, please?

Questo non funziona, me lo può riparare per favore?

black-and-white film	pellicola in bianco e nero
colour film	pellicola a colori
film camera	cinepresa
film speed	sensibilità del film
flash	il flash
flashcube	il cuboflash
lens	la lente
objective	obiettivo
shutter release (self timer) .	scatto
shutter	l'otturatore *m*
telephoto lens	teleobiettivo

SHOE SHOP | NEGOZIO DI CALZATURE

I'd like a pair of ...shoes.

Vorrei un paio di scarpe ...

They're too narrow/wide.

Sono troppo strette/larghe.

And a tube of shoe cream/ a pair of shoelaces, please.

Anche un lucido da scarpe/un paio di laccetti, per favore.

boots	gli stivali
children's shoes	le scarpe da bambini
flat shoes	le scarpe basse
sandals	i sandali
shoes	le scarpe
shoe brush	spazzola da scarpe
shoecream	lucido per scarpe
shoe size	numero di scarpe
trainers	le scarpe da ginnastica

STATIONER'S / ARTICOLI DI CARTOLERIA

I'd like ...	Vorrei ...
an English newspaper.	un giornale inglese.
a magazine.	una rivista.
a guide.	una guida turistica.

ballpoint pen	la biro
envelope	busta
eraser	gomma
fountain pen	penna stilografica
gift wrap	carta da regalo
glue	colla
guide	il guida
magazine	periodico, rivista, rotocalco
map	carta geografica
map of walks	mappa dei sentieri
newspaper	il giornale
notepad	blocco per appunti, il bloc-notes
novel	romanzo
paper	carta
paperback	libro tascabile
pencil	matita
picture postcard	cartolina illustrata
playing cards	carte da gioco
road map	carta automobilistica
rubber	gomma
Sellotape	lo scotch®, nastro adesivo
sketchbook	album da disegno
stamp	francobollo
town map	pianta della città
writing-paper	carta da lettere

TOBACCONIST'S / TABACCHI

A packet/carton of filter-tipped/plain ... cigarettes, please.	Un pacchetto/Una stecca di ... con/senza filtro, per favore.
Ten cigars/cigarillos, please.	Dieci sigari/sigarillos, per favore.
A packet/tin of cigarette/pipe tobacco, please.	Un pacchetto/Una scatola di tabacco per sigarette/ per la pipa, per favore.
A box of matches, please.	Una scatola di fiammiferi, per favore.
A lighter, please.	Un accendino, per favore.

A double room, please

Can you recommend ...,
please?
  a hotel
  a guest-house
  a bed-and-breakfast
  place

Scusi signora/signorina/signore,
potrebbe consigliarmi ...
  un albergo
  una pensione?
  una camera privata?

Is there a youth hostel/a
camping-site here?

C'è un ostello della gioventù/un
camping qui?

HOTEL

RECEPTION DESK | L'ACCETTAZIONE, LA RECEPTION

I've reserved a room. My
name's ...

Ho prenotato una camera.
Il mio nome è ...

Have you got any vacan-
cies?
  ... for one night.
  ... for two days/a week.

Ha camere libere?

  ... per una notte.
  ... per due giorni/per una settimana.

No, I'm afraid we're full
up.

No, purtroppo è tutto esaurito.

Yes, what sort of room
would you like?
  a single room
  a double room
  with a shower
  with a bath
  a quiet room
  with a view of the sea
  at the front

Sì, che tipo di camera desidera?

  una singola
  una doppia
  con doccia
  con bagno
  una camera tranquilla
  con vista sul mare
  che dà sulla strada

Can I see the room?	Posso vedere la camera?
Can you put another bed/ a cot in the room?	Si può aggiungere un altro letto/un lettino (per bambini)?
How much is the room with ...	Quanto costa la camera ...
breakfast?	con la prima colazione?
breakfast and evening meal?	a mezza pensione?
full board?	a pensione completa?
Where can I park the car?	Dove posso lasciare la macchina?
In our garage/car-park.	Nel nostro garage/parcheggio.
Has the hotel got a swimming-pool/a private beach?	L'albergo ha una piscina/una spiaggia riservata?
What time's breakfast?	Da che ora si può fare colazione?
Where's the dining room?	Dov'è la sala da pranzo?
I'd like breakfast in my room at ... o'clock, please.	Mi faccia portare, per favore, la colazione in camera alle ...

Breakfast: see FOOD & DRINK, Menu p. 35

Please wake me at ... o'clock in the morning.	Mi svegli domattina alle ..., per favore.
My key, please.	Per favore, la mia chiave.

COMPLAINTS — RECLAMI

The room hasn't been cleaned.	La camera non è stata pulita.
The shower...	La doccia ...
The flush...	Lo sciacquone ...
The heating ...	Il riscaldamento ...
The light ... doesn't work.	La luce ... non funziona.
There's no (warm) water.	Non c'è acqua (calda).
The toilet/wash-basin is blocked up.	Il gabinetto/Il lavandino è intasato.

DEPARTURE	PARTENZA

I'm leaving this evening/ tomorrow at ... o'clock.	Parto stasera/domani alle ...
I'd like my bill, please.	Mi prepari il conto, per favore.
Do you accept ...	Accetta ...
English money?	denaro inglese?
eurocheques?	eurocheques?
credit cards?	carte di credito?
traveller's cheques?	assegni turistici, traveller's cheques?
Thank you very much for everything. Goodbye!	Grazie di tutto. Arrivederci.

adapter	spina di adattamento
air-conditioning	aria condizionata
babysitting service	assistenza ai bambini
balcony	il balcone
bathroom	bagno
bath tub	vasca da bagno
bed	letto
bed-linen	biancheria da letto
bedside table	comodino
blanket	coperta di lana
breakfast	la colazione
breakfast-room	sala per la colazione
chambermaid	cameriera
to clean	pulire
cot	lettino (per bambini)
cupboard	armadio
dining-room	sala da pranzo
dinner	cena
floor, storey	piano
full board	la pensione completa
guest house	la pensione
half board	la mezza pensione
heating	riscaldamento
high season	alta stagione *f*
key	la chiave
lamp	lampada
lift, elevator	l'ascensore *m*
low season	bassa stagione *f*
lunch	pranzo, il desinare
mirror	specchio
pillow	cuscino
plug	spina
porter	il portiere
radio	la radio

reading-lamp	lampada del comodino
reception	atrio, l'accettazione *f*, la reception
registration	l'accettazione *f*
reservation	la prenotazione
room	camera
safe	la cassaforte
shower	doccia
(wall-)socket	presa
tap	rubinetto
television, TV	il televisore
television lounge	camera della televisione
toilet	gabinetto
toilet-paper	carta igienica
towel	asciugamano
window	finestra
overnight stay	pernottamento
washbasin	lavandino
water	acqua
cold water	acqua fredda
warm water	acqua calda

RENTED ACCOMODATION

Is electricity and water included in the price?	L'acqua e la luce sono comprese nel prezzo d'affitto?
Are pets allowed?	Si possono portare animali?
Where can we pick up the keys to the house/the flat?	Dove possiamo ritirare le chiavi della casa/dell'appartamento?
Do we have to clean the flat before we leave?	Spetta a noi il lavoro di pulizia finale?

additional costs, extras	le spese (accessorie)
bedroom	camera da letto
bungalow	il bungalow
bunk bed	letto a castello
coffee machine	macchina del caffè
cooker, stove	cucina economica
day of arrival	giorno d'arrivo
electricity	la corrente
flat	appartamento
holiday camp	centro vacanze
holiday flat	appartamento per le vacanze
holiday home	casa per le vacanze

ACCOMMODATION

kitchenette	cucinino, cucinotto
landlord/landlady	il padrone/la padrone di casa
living-room	soggiorno
pets	gli animali domestici
refrigerator, fridge	frigorifero
rent	affitto, noleggio
rubbish	immondizia
studio couch	divano a letto
tea towel	strofinaccio per asciugare i piatti
to let, to rent	affittare, noleggiare
toaster	il tostapane
washing machine	la lavatrice

CAMPING

Have you got room for another caravan/tent?	C'è posto per una roulotte/una tenda?
How much does it cost per day and person?	Quanto si paga al giorno a persona?
What's the charge for ... the car? the caravan? the camper van? the tent?	Quanto si paga per ... l'auto? la roulotte? il camper? la tenda?
We'll be staying for ... days/weeks.	Rimaniamo ... giorni/settimane.
Is there a food-store here?	C'è un negozio di alimentari?
Where are the ... toilets? washrooms?	Dove sono ... i servizi igienici? i lavandini?
Are there electric points here?	C'è una presa di corrente?
Is it 220 or 110 volts?	Qui la corrente è da 220 o da 110 volt?
Where can I exchange/hire gas canisters?	Dove posso cambiare/affittare le bombole di gas?

booking	preavviso
to camp	campeggiare
camper	il camper
camping	camping *m*, campeggio

camping guide	guida dei campeggi
camping-site	campeggio
caravan	la roulotte
children's playground	campo da gioco per bambini
cooker	fornello
drinking water	acqua potabile
electric point	presa di corrente
electricity	la corrente
gas canister	bombola di gas
gas-cooker	fornello a gas
to hire	prestare
hire charge	tariffa di noleggio
(hire) charge	tassa per l'uso
paraffin lamp	lampada a petrolio
plug	spina
sink	lavandino per i piatti
tent peg	picchetto
tent	tenda
tentpole	palo da tenda
tent tie	laccio da tenda
(wall-)socket	presa
water	acqua

YOUTH HOSTEL

Can I hire ...?	Mi può noleggiare ...
... bed-linen?	... la biancheria da letto?
... a sleeping-bag?	... un sacco a pelo?

The front door is locked at midnight.	Il portone d'ingresso viene chiuso alle ore 24.

day room	sala di soggiorno
dormitory	dormitorio
hall of residence	casa dello studente
membership card	tessera di socio
sleeping-bag	sacco a pelo
washroom	stanzino da bagno
youth hostel	ostello della gioventù
youth hostelling card	tessera per gli ostelli della gioventù

Out on the town

BAR/DISCOTHEQUE/ NIGHT-CLUB	BAR/DISCOTECA/ NIGHT-CLUB
What can we do here in the evenings?	Che cosa si puo' fare qui la sera?
Is there a nice pub here?	C'è una trattoria accogliente da queste parti?
Where can we go dancing?	Dove si può andare a ballare?
Is evening dress required?	È richiesto l'abito da sera?
One drink is included in the price of admission.	Il biglietto d'ingresso comprende una consumazione.
A whisky and soda, please.	Un whisky e soda, per favore.
The same again.	Un'altra/Un altro, per favore.
This round's on me.	Stavolta offro io.
Shall we (have another) dance?	Balliamo (ancora)?

band	complesso
bar	il bar
bouncer	il portiere
casino	casinò
to dance	ballare
dance band	orchestra
dance music	musica da ballo
discotheque	discoteca
folklore	il folclore
folk-dances	danze folcloristiche
folksong	canto folclore
gambling arcade	sala giochi
to go out	uscire
live music	musica dal vivo
night-club	il night-club
pub	osteria, trattoria
show	lo show

Elbows up!

"alzare il gomito" (literally *"to lift one's elbow"*) means *to get drunk.*

Have you got a diary of events for this week?	Ha un programma delle manifestazioni di questa settimana?
What's on (at the theatre) tonight?	Che cosa c'è al teatro stasera?
Can you recommend a good play?	Mi può consigliare una buona rappresentazione teatrale?
When does the performance start?	Quando comincia lo spettacolo?
Where can I get tickets?	Dove si prendono i biglietti?
Two tickets for this evening/tomorrow evening, please.	Due biglietti per stasera/domani sera, per favore.
Two seats at ..., please.	Per favore due biglietti da ... lire.
Can I have a programme, please?	Mi può dare un programma, per favore?
Where's the cloakroom?	Dov'è il guardaroba?

advance booking	prevendita
ballet	balletto
box office	cassa
calendar of events	calendario delle manifestazioni
cinema	il cinema
circus	circo
cloakroom	il guardaroba
composer	compositore
concert	concerto
conductor	il direttore d'orchestra
festival	il festival, festa
film, movie	il film
music hall	il varietà
musical	il musical, commedia musicale
opera	opera
performance	spettacolo
play	commedia
premiere	prima
programme (of events) . . .	il programma
programme (brochure) . . .	opuscolo del programma
theatre	teatro
ticket	biglietto
variety theatre	il varietà

On the beach

AT THE SWIMMING POOL/ ON THE BEACH	IN PISCINA/SULLA SPIAGGIA

Is there ... here?	C'è ...
an open-air pool	una piscina all'aperto?
an indoor pool	una piscina coperta?
thermal baths	un bagno termale?

Swimmers only!	Per soli nuotatori!
No diving!	Vietato tuffarsi!
No swimming!	Vietato bagnarsi!

Are there sea-urchins/ jellyfish here?	Ci sono ricci/meduse?
Is there a strong current?	È molto forte la corrente?
Is it dangerous for children?	È pericoloso per i bambini?
When's low tide?	Quando viene la bassa marea?
When's high tide?	Quando viene l'alta marea?
I'd like to rent ...	Vorrei noleggiare ...
a boat.	una barca.
a pair of water-skis.	un paio di sci nautici.
How much is it per hour/ day?	Quanto costa all'ora/al giorno?

SPORT	SPORT

What sports facilities are there here?	Quali sport si possono praticare qui?
Is there ... here?	C'è ...
a golf-course	un campo da golf?
a tennis court	un campo da tennis?
a race-course	un ippodromo?

Where can I go fishing?	Dove si può pescare?
I'd like to hire a bike for ... days/for a week.	Vorrei noleggiare per ... giorni/una settimana una bicicletta.
I'd like to go for a hike in the mountains.	Vorrei fare una gita in montagna.
Can you show me an interesting route on the map?	Mi può indicare un itinerario interessante sulla carta?
Where can I hire ...?	Dove posso noleggiare ...?
I'd like to attend a ... course.	Vorrei fare un corso di ...
Can I play too?	Posso giocare anch'io?

activity holidays	vacanza attiva
airbed	materasso pneumatico
athletics	atletica leggera
attendant	bagnino
badminton	il badminton, gioco del volano
badminton	volano
ball	palla, il pallone; (dance) ballo
basketball	il Basketball, pallacanestro
beginner	il principiante
boat hire	noleggio di barche
cable railway	funivia, la funicolare
canoe	canoa
chairlift	seggiovia
championship	campionato
contest	gara
course	corso; (route) rotta
crazy golf	il minigolf
crew	squadra
cross-country skiing	lo sci di fondo
to cycle	andare in bicicletta
cycle racing	corsa ciclistica
cycle tour	gita in bicicletta
darts	tiro a segno con i dardi
deck chair	sedia a sdraio
deep-sea fishing	pesca d'alto mare
defeat	sconfitta
to dive	nuotare sott'acqua
diving equipment	attrezzatura da palombaro
diving goggles	gli occhiali da immersione
diving-board	trampolino
draw (tie)	pari
fishing licence	licenza di pesca
fishing rod	pescare

fitness centre	centro ginnico
fitness training	allenamento per migliorare la forma
football	calcio
football ground	campo da gioco (del calcio)
football match	partita di calcio
football team	squadra di calcio
funicular	funivia, la funicolare
game	partita
gliding	volo a vela
goal	porta, il goal
goalkeeper	il portiere
golf	il golf
golf club	mazza da golf
golf course	campo da golf
gymnastics	ginnastica
half, first/second ~	primo/secondo tempo
handball	palla a mano
hiking	camminare
horse	cavallo
ice-hockey	l'hockey su ghiaccio *m*
ice-rink	pista per pattinaggio su ghiaccio
ice-skates	i pattini
to jog	fare jogging
jogging	il jogging
lifeguard	bagnino
to lose	perdere
match	partita
motorboat	motoscafo
net	la rete
ninepin bowling	gioco dei birilli
non-swimmer	non nuotatore
nudist beach	spiaggia per nudisti
open-air pool	piscina all'aperto
parachuting	paracadutismo
path	sentiero
pedal boat	pattino a pedali
private beach	spiaggia privata
programme	il programma
race	corsa
referee	arbitro
regatta	regata
result	risultato
to ride, to go riding	cavalcare
ride	cavalcata
riding	l'equitazione *f;* ippica
rock-climbing	alpinismo
rowing/canoeing	canottaggio
rowing-boat	barca a remi

rubber dinghy	canotto pneumatico
sailing	vela
sailing-boat	barca a vela
sand	sabbia
sand-dune	duna
sauna	sauna
shower	doccia
ski	lo sci
ski tow	sciovia, lo ski-lift
skiing	sciare
sledge	slitta
snorkel	il respiratore di superficie
soccer	calcio
solarium	solario
sports ground	campo sportivo
sportsman/-woman	sportivo/sportiva
squash	lo squash
start	partenza
sunshade	l'ombrellone *m*
to surf	praticare il surfing
surfboard	tavoletta per il surf
surfing	il surf
swimmer	il nuotatore
swimming	nuoto
swimming pool	piscina
table tennis	il ping-pong
tennis	il tennis
tennis racket	racchetta
ticket	biglietto d'ingresso
ticket office	cassa
toboggan	slitta
to go tobogganing	andare in slitta
tyre	il salvagente
volleyball	la pallavolo
water polo	pallanuoto
water wing	i bracciali *pl* salvagente
to win	vincere
win	vittoria
windbreak	frangivento
victory	vittoria

Looking after the kids

Do you have children's portions?	Si può avere la mezza-porzione per i bambini?
Could you please warm up the bottle?	Mi potrebbe riscaldare il biberon, per favore?
Do you have a mothers' and babies' room?	C'è un fasciatoio?
Where can I breast feed?	Dove posso allattare?
Please bring another high chair.	Mi porti ancora un seggiolone, per favore.
Is there a children's play area?	C'è un campo da gioco per i bambini?

baby food	l'alimentazione *f* infantile
baby's changing table	fasciatoio
babysitter	baby-sitter
babysitting service	assistenza ai bambini
bottle warmer	scaldabiberon
child reduction	riduzione per bambini
child's safety seat	seggiolino per l'auto
children's hospital	ospedale dei bambini
dummy	ciuccio, succhietto
paddling pool	piscina per bambini
playground	campo giochi
playmates	compagni di gioco
toys	giocattoli
tyre	salvagente
water wing	il bracciale

Making Friends

What is your name?	Come ti chiami?
My name's ...	Mi chiamo ...
Where are you from?	Di dove sei?
I come from ...	Sono di ...
Do you want to play with me?	Vuoi giocare con me?

beach
spiaggia

castle
castello

changing room
cabina

sunshade
ombrellone

ice-cream
gelato

lifeguard
bagnino

sailing-boat
barca a vela

shovel
paletta

towel
asciugamano

raft
zattera

ball
palla

water
acqua

TRAVELLING WITH CHILDREN

baker's
panificio

car
macchina

street
via, strada

police
polizia

lights
semaforo

dog
cane

accident
incidente

bike
biciclett

fire-brigade
vigili del fuoco

tram
tram

The Essentials

BANK/EXCHANGE	BANCA/CAMBIO
Where's the nearest bank/ bureau de change?	Scusi, dove posso trovare una banca/ un'agenzia di cambio?
I'd like to change ... pounds (dollars) into lire.	Vorrei cambiare queste sterline (questi dollari) in Lire.
What's the current exchange rate?	Quant'è oggi il cambio?
How many lire do I get for a hundred pounds/dollars?	A quante lire corrispondono 100 sterline/dollari?
I'd like to change this traveller's-cheque/euro-cheque.	Vorrei riscuotere questo traveller's-chèque/eurocheque.
What is the maximum I can cash on one cheque?	Qual è l'importo massimo per la ris-cossione dell'assegno?
Can I see your cheque card, please?	La carta assegni, per favore.
May I see your passport/ identity card, please?	Posso vedere il Suo passaporto/la Sua carta d'identità?
Sign here, please.	Firmi qui, per favore.
Go to the cashdesk, please.	Si accomodi alla cassa, per favore.

American dollars .... dollari americani
amount .... importo
bank .... banca
bank account .... conto bancario
bank code number ...... numero guida bancario
banknote .... banconota
bureau de change .... agenzia di cambio
cash .... in contanti
cashpoint .... cassa automatica prelievi, il banco-mat, sportello automatico
to change .... cambiare
change .... gli spiccioli, moneta
cheque .... assegno
cheque card .... carta assegni

70

coin	moneta
counter	sportello
credit card	carta di credito
currency	valuta
English pounds	sterline inglesi
eurocheque	l'eurocheque *m*
exchange	cambio
exchange rate	corso dei cambi
form	modulo
money	denaro
to pay out	pagare
payment	pagamento
pin number	numero segreto
rate of exchange	cambio
signature	firma
Swiss franc(s)	franco svizzero
traveller's cheque	assegno turistico, il traveller's chèque

CUSTOMS/ PASSPORT CONTROL	DOGANA/CONTROLLO PASSAPORTI
Your passport, please.	Il Suo passaporto, per favore!
Your passport has expired.	Il Suo passaporto è scaduto.
Have you got a visa?	Ha il visto?
Can I get a visa here?	Mi potete rilasciare qui il visto?
Have you got anything to declare?	Ha niente da dichiarare?
No, I've only got a few presents.	No, ho soltanto alcuni regali.
Pull over to the right/the left, please.	Si metta lì a destra/a sinistra.
Open the boot (*Am* trunk)/this case, please.	Apra, per favore, il bagagliaio/questa valigia.
Do I have to pay duty on this?	Devo sdoganare questo?

border	frontiera, il confine
Christian name	il nome
customs	dogana
customs check	ispezione *(f)* doganale
date of birth	data di nascita
driving-licence	la patente
duty	dogana
duty-free	esente da dazio doganale
endorsement	visto

to enter the country	entrare (in un paese)
export	l'esportazione f, l'esecuzione f
first name	il nome
identity card	carta d'identità
import	l'importazione f
to leave the country	partire (per l'estero)
liable to duty	soggetto a dazio doganale
maiden name	il nome da ragazza
marital status	stato di famiglia
married	sposato/sposata
national identity sticker ..	targa di nazionalità
nationality	nazionalità
number plate	targa
passport	passaporto
passport control	controllo passaporti
place of birth	luogo di nascita
place of residence	domicilio
rabies	idrofobia
single	*(male)* celibe; *(female)* nubile
surname	il cognome
valid	valido
visa	visto
widow/widower	vedova/vedovo

DOCTOR	MEDICO

At the doctor's

Dal medico

Can you recommend a good ...	Mi può consigliare un buon ...
doctor?	medico?
dentist?	dentista?
dermatologist?	dermatologo?
ear, nose and throat specialist?	otorinolaringoiatra?
eye specialist?	oculista?
GP?	medico generico?
gynaecologist?	ginecologo?
neurologist?	neurologo?
pediatrician?	pediatra?
urologist?	urologo?
Where's his surgery?	Dov'è il suo ambulatorio?
What's the trouble?	Che disturbi ha?
I've got a temperature.	Ho la febbre.
I often feel sick.	Spesso mi sento male.
I often feel faint/dizzy.	Spesso mi gira la testa.
I fainted.	Sono svenuto/svenuta.

I've got a bad cold.	Sono molto raffreddato/a.
I've got ...	Ho ...
a headache.	mal di testa.
a sore throat.	mal di gola.
a cough.	la tosse.
I've been stung.	Sono stato punto/punta.
I've been bitten.	Sono stato morso/morsa.
I've got diarrhoea./I'm constipated.	Soffro di diarrea/costipazione.
I've hurt myself.	Mi sono fatto/fatta male.
Where does it hurt?	Dove fa male?
I've got a pain here.	Ho dei dolori qui.
I'm a diabetic.	Sono diabetico/diabetica.
I'm pregnant.	Sono incinta.
It's nothing serious.	Non è niente di grave.
Can you give me/prescribe something for ...?	Mi può dare/prescrivere qualcosa contro ...?
I usually take ...	Di solito prendo ...

At the dentist's   Dal dentista

I've got (terrible) toothache.	Ho (un forte) mal di denti.
This tooth (at the top/bottom/front/back) hurts.	Questo dente (di sopra/di sotto/davanti/in fondo) fa male.
I've lost a filling.	La piombatura è andata via.
I've broken a tooth.	Mi si è rotto un dente.
I'll have to fill it.	Lo devo otturare.
It'll have to come out.	Devo estrarlo.
I'd like an injection, please.	Mi faccia una puntura, per favore.
I don't want an injection.	Non mi faccia la puntura, per favore.

In hospital   In ospedale

How long will I have to stay here?	Per quanto tempo devo stare qui?
When can I get up?	Quando potrò alzarmi?

ACCETTAZIONE (Reception)	SALA D'ASPETTO (Waiting room)	AMBULATORIO (Surgery)

abdomen	l'addome *m*
abscess	ascesso
Aids	Aids
allergy	allergia
anaesthetic	anestesia
ankle	caviglia
appendix	l'appendice *f*
arm	braccio
artifical limb	la protesi
asthma	l'asma *m/f*
back	schiena
backache	il dolore alla schiena
bandage	fascia
bladder	vescica
to bleed	sanguinare
blood	il sangue
blood group	gruppo sanguigno
blood pressure	la pressione sanguigna
blood-poisoning	setticemia
bone	osso
bowel movement	le feci
brain	cervello
breast	petto
to breathe	respirare
broken	rotto
bronchitis	la bronchite
bruise	la contusione
burn	l'ustione *f*
bypass (operation)	bypass
cancer	cancro
cardiac arrest	infarto, attacco cardiaco
cavity	la carie
chickenpox	varicella
circulatory disorder	disturbi circolatori
cold	il raffreddore
to catch a cold	prendere freddo, raffreddarsi
colic	colica
collarbone	clavicola
concussion	la commozione cerebrale
constipation	la costipazione, stitichezza
contagious	contagioso
contusion	la contusione
cough	la tosse
cramp	crampo
cut	ferita da taglio
diabetes	il diabete
diarrhoea	diarrea
difficulty in breathing	difficoltà di respirazione
digestion	la digestione

to disinfect	disinfettare
dizziness	le vertigini
to dress	fasciare
dressing	fasciatura
ear	orecchio
eardrum	membrana del timpano
examination	l'esame *m*
to extract	togliere, estrarre
eye	occhio
face	faccia
fainting	svenimento
fever	la febbre
filling	piombatura
finger	dito
fit of shivering	i brividi
flu	influenza
food-poisoning	l'intossicazione *f* da alimenti
foot	il piede
fracture	frattura, frattura ossea
gall-bladder	la cistifellea
German measles	rosolia
gullet	esofago
hand	la mano
head	testa
headache	il mal di testa
hearing	udito
heart	il cuore
heart attack	infarto, attacco cardiaco
heart defect	difetto cardiaco
heart trouble	i disturbi cardiaci
hernia	l'ernia; ernia inguinale
hip	anca
hospital	l'ospedale *m*
to hurt *(to be painful)*	far male
to hurt *(to injure)*	ferire
ill	malato
illness	malattia
indigestion	l'indigestione *f*
infection	l'infezione *f*
inflammation	l'infiammazione *f*
~ of the middle ear	l'otite *f*
injection	l'iniezione *f*, puntura
to injure	ferire
injury	ferita
intestines	intestino
jaundice	itterizia
jaw	mascella
joint	l'articolazione *f*
kidney stone	calcolo renale

knee	ginocchio
leg	gamba
lip	labbro
liver	fegato
lumbago	la lombaggine
lungs	il polmone
measles	morbillo
medical insurance card	buono per le cure mediche
menstruation	la mestruazione
migraine	emicrania
miscarriage	aborto
mouth	bocca
mumps	gli orecchioni
muscle	muscolo
nausea	nausea
neck	collo
nephritis	la nefrite
nerve	nervo
nervous	nervoso
nose	naso
nurse	infermiera
operation	l'operazione f
pacemaker	il cardiostimolatore, il pacemaker
pain	i dolori
painful, to be ~	far male
paralysis	la paralisi
poisoning	avvelenamento
polio	la polio(melite)
practice	ambulatorio
pregnancy	gravidanza
to prescribe	prescrivere
pulled ligament/muscle	stiramento
pulse	polso
pus	il pus
rash	l'eruzione f cutanea, l'esantema m
rheumatism	i reumatismi
rib	costola
rupture	ernia inguinale
salmonellae	la salmonellosi
scan	l'esame m con ultrasuoni, ecografia
scar	la cicatrice
scarlet fever	scarlattina
sciatica	sciatica
sexual organs	gli organi genitali
shin	tibia
shoulder	spalla
sick	malato
sinusitis	la sinusite
skin	la pelle

skull	cranio
sleeplessness	insonnia
smallpox	vaiolo
sore throat	mal di gola
spine	spina dorsale, colonna vertebrale
sprained	slogato
sting	punto, puntura
stomach	il ventre
stomach	stomaco
stomach-ache	il mal di stomaco
stroke	apoplessia cerebrale, colpo apoplettico
sunstroke	colpo di sole
surgeon	chirurgo
surgery opening times	orario di visita
swelling	il gonfiore, la tumefazione
swollen	gonfio
syringe	siringa
to take out	togliere, estrarre
temperature	la febbre
tetanus	tetano
throat	gola
toe	dito del piede
tongue	lingua
tonsils	le tonsille
tooth	il dente
toothache	mal di denti
torn ligament	strappo dei legamenti
typhoid	tifo
ulcer	ulcera
unconscious	privo di sensi
urine	urina
vaccination	la vaccinazione
veneral disease	malattia venerea
virus	il virus
to vomit	vomitare
waiting room	sala d'aspetto
ward	reparto
wind	flatulenza
wound	ferita
wrist	polso
X-ray	radiografare

LOCAL TRANSPORT — TRASPORTI PUBBLICI

Excuse me, where's the nearest ...	Dov'è la prossima ...
bus stop?	fermata dell'autobus?
tram stop?	fermata del tram?
underground station?	stazione della metropolitana?

Which line goes to ...?	Qual è la linea che va a ...?
What time does the bus leave?	Quando parte l'autobus?
Where does the bus leave from?	Da dove parte l'autobus?
Where do I have to get out/change?	Dove devo scendere/cambiare?
Will you tell me when we're there, please.	Mi dice, per favore quando devo scendere?
Where can I buy a ticket?	Dove si comprano i biglietti?
To ..., please.	Un biglietto per ..., per favore.

bus	l'autobus *m*
to buy a ticket	comprare un biglietto
departure	partenza
driver	il conducente
fare	prezzo del biglietto
to get on	salire
to get out	scendere
inspector	il controllore
one-day travelcard	biglietto giornaliero
to press the button	premere il pulsante
road	strada, via
stop	fermata
street	strada, via
terminus	il capolinea
ticket	biglietto
ticket machine	il distributore automatico di biglietti
timetable	orario
tram	il tram
travelcard	abbonamento per tutta la rete
underground	metropolitana
weekly season ticket	abbonamento settimanale

LOST-PROPERTY OFFICE | UFFICIO OGGETTI SMARRITI

Where's the lost-property office, please?	Per favore, dov'è l'ufficio oggetti smarriti?
I've lost ...	Ho perso ...
I left my handbag on the train.	Ho lasciato la (mia) borsa sul treno.
Please let me know if it's handed in.	Per favore, se viene riconsegnata, me lo faccia sapere.
Here's the address of my hotel address.	Ecco l'indirizzo del mio albergo.

POLICE	POLIZIA
Where's the nearest police station, please?	Dov'è il commissariato di polizia più vicino?
I'd like to report an accident/a theft.	Vorrei denunciare un incidente/un furto.
My ... has been stolen.	Mi è stato rubato .../ Mi è stata rubata ...
handbag	la borsa.
wallet	il portafoglio.
camera	la macchina fotografica.
car	la macchina.
bike	la bicicletta.
My car has been broken into.	La mia macchina è stata forzata.
... has been stolen from my car.	Dalla mia macchina è stato rubato ...
I've lost ...	Ho perso ...
My son/daughter has been missing since ...	Mio figlio/Mia figlia è scomparso/ scomparsa da ...
Can you help me, please?	Mi può aiutare, per favore?
We'll look into the matter.	Ce ne occuperemo.
I've got nothing to do with it.	Non ho niente a che fare con questa faccenda.
Your name and address, please.	Il Suo nome e indirizzo, per favore.
Get in touch with the British/American consulate.	Per favore, si rivolga al consolato britannico/americano.

to arrest	arrestare
assault	l'aggressione *f*
to beat up	picchiare
to bother	infastidire
to break into/open	forzare, scassinare
car keys	la chiave della macchina
car radio	l'autoradio *f*
cheque	assegno
cheque card	carta assegni
to confiscate	sequestrare
crime	delitto
court	tribunale
documents	i documenti
drugs	gli stupefacenti
identity card	carta d'identità
judge	giudice *m f*
lawyer	avvocato/avvocatessa

lose	perdere
money	denaro
mugging	l'aggressione *f*
papers	i documenti
passport	passaporto
to pester	infastidire
pickpocket	borsaiolo, lo scippatore
police	polizia
policeman/policewoman	l'agente *m f*; il vigile/la vigilessa
prison	la prigione
purse	il portamonete
rape	violenza(carnale), stupro
to report	denunciare
theft	furto
thief	ladro
wallet	portafoglio

POST OFFICE / UFFICIO POSTALE

Where's ... the nearest post office? the nearest post-box?	Per favore, dov'è ... l'ufficio postale più vicino? la cassetta postale più vicina?
How much does a letter/ postcard ... to Great Britain to America cost?	Quanto costa una lettera/una cartolina illustrata per ... la Gran Bretagna? America?
I'd like to send this letter ... by airmail. express.	Questa lettera ..., per favore. posta aerea per espresso
How long does a letter to Great Britain/America take?	Quanto tempo impiega una lettera per la Gran Bretagna/America?

address	indirizzo
addressee	destinatario
by airmail	via aerea
charge	tariffa
collection	levata
counter	sportello
destination	la destinazione
envelope	busta
express letter	espresso
fee	tariffa
to fill in	compilare
form	modulo
letter	lettera
main post office	posta centrale

parcel	pacco
to post	spedire
post code	CAP (codice di avviamento postale)
post office	ufficio postale
postage	affrancatura
post-box	cassetta postale
postcard	cartolina postale
to send on	recapitare
sender	il mittente
special issue stamp	l'emissione f speciale
to stamp	affrancare
stamp	francobollo
weight	peso

TAXI / TASSÌ

Where's the nearest taxi rank?	Dove trovo un tassì?
To the station.	Alla stazione.
To the ... Hotel.	All'albergo ...
To ... Street.	In via ...
To ..., please.	A ..., per favore.
How much will it cost to ...?	Quanto costa andare a ...?
Could you stop here, please?	Si fermi qui.
That's for you.	Questo è per Lei.
taxi-driver	il tassista
taxi rank	posteggio di taxi
tip	mancia

TELEPHONING / TELEFONARE

Where's the nearest phone box?	Dov'è la cabina telefonica più vicina?
Can I have ..., please? a token a phonecard	Mi potrebbe dare ...? un gettone una carta telefonica
Have you got a ... telephone directory?	Ha un elenco telefonico di ...?
What's the national code for ...?	Qual è il prefisso di ...?
I'd like to make a long distance call to ...	Per favore, un'interurbana per ...

I'd like to make a reverse charge call.	Vorrei annunciare una telefonata a carico del ricevente.
Go to booth number ...	Vada nella cabina numero ...
This is ... speaking.	Qui parla ...
Hello, who's speaking?	Pronto, con chi parlo?
Can I speak to Mr/Mrs/Miss ..., please?	Scusi, potrei parlare con il signor/la signora/la signorina ...?
Speaking.	Sono io.
I'm sorry, he's/she's not here.	Mi dispiace, ma non c'è.
Can he/she call you back?	La posso far richiamare?
Yes, my number's ...	Sì, il mio numero è ...
Would you tell him/her that I called?	Gli/Le potrebbe dire che ho chiamato, per favore?

to answer the phone	rispondere al telefono
busy	occupato
call	la conversazione
charge	tariffa
to dial	formare il numero
to dial direct	raggiungere in teleselezione
directory enquiries	informazioni
international call	la comunicazione internazionale
local call	telefonata urbana
long-distance call	interurbana
national code	prefisso
payphone	telefono a gettone
phone box	cabina telefonica
phone call	telefonata
phone number	numero telefonico
phonecard	carta telefonica
reverse charge call	la comunicazione telefonica a carico del ricevente
to ring up	telefonare
telephone	telefono
telephone directory	elenco telefonico
unit	scatto

Warning!

The following are some of the expressions you should be aware of so that if they come up in conversation you have some idea what the person you are talking to might be thinking of you! Be warned: the publishers are not responsible for the consequences of any improper use on your part!

Che imbecille!	What a fool!
Che deficiente!	What a moron!
Che cretino!	What a cretin / an idiot!
Stronzo!	Shit! Turd!
Coglione!	Pillock! Arsehole!
Testa di cazzo!	Dickhead!
Scemo!	Silly twit!
Maledizione!	Damn (it)!
Col cavolo che lo faccio! / Un corno!	Like hell (I will)! Not on your life!
Me ne frego!	I don't give a damn!
Che merda!	What an arsehole!
Cazzate!	Bullshit!
Non dire minchiate!	Don't talk crap!
Vai al diavolo! / Vai a quel paese!	Go to hell!
Vaffanculo!	Fuck off!
Non capisci un cazzo!	You don't know / understand a bloody thing!
Rompere i coglioni / le palle a qualcuno	to piss someone off

"To have", "To be" and other verbs

- Because the verb endings already indicate the subject, personal pronouns are not used (eg "**abbiamo** tempo" – "we have time") except when you want to emphasize who the subject is.
- The polite form in Italian is:
  - the 3rd person singular when addressing one person (eg "**ha** tempo, signor Neri?" – "do you have time, Mr Neri?")
  - the 2nd person plural or, in very formal circumstances, the 3rd person plural when addressing more than one person (eg "**avete** tempo/ **hanno** tempo, signori?" – "do you (pl.) have time?")

avere, essere

	avere	to have	essere	to be
io	ho	I have	sono	I am
tu	hai	you have	sei	you are
lui		he has		he is
lei	ha	she has	è	she is
lei		you *(formal)* have		you *(formal)* are
noi	abbiamo	we have	siamo	we are
voi	avete	you have	siete	you are
loro	hanno	they have, you *(very formal, pl.)* have	sono	they are, you *(very formal, pl.)* are

- c'è there is – ci sono there are

Regular verbs

Italian verbs are divided into three groups, conjugated according to their infinitive endings:

	Verbs ending -are		-ere	-ire	
	parlare to speak, to talk		vendere to sell	partire to leave	capire to understand
io	parlo	I speak	vendo	parto	capisco
tu	parli	you speak	vendi	parti	capisci
lui		he speaks			
lei	parla	she speaks	vende	parte	capisce
lei		you speak			
noi	parliamo	we speak	vendiamo	partiamo	capiamo
voi	parlate	you speak	vendete	partite	capite
loro	parlano	they speak you speak	vendono	partono	capiscono

ENGLISH-ITALIAN DICTIONARY

The 1333 most important words

The numbers following the Italian translations refer to the relevant sections. For tips on pronunciation see page 4.

A

to be able to essere capace di, potere
about *(approximately)* circa, quasi, verso; *(place)* intorno a; *(relating to)* a proposito di
accident incidente *(m)*, disgrazia → p. 19; **to have an ~** avere un incidente
accommodation alloggio → p. 55
to accompany accompagnare
across attraverso
activity attività
addition, in ~ supplementare, in più
additional supplementare, in più
addressee destinatario → p. 80
address indirizzo → p. 80
Adriatic Sea l'Adriatico
adult adulto/adulta
advance, in ~ in anticipo
advance booking prevendita → p. 62
to advise consigliare
affair *(event)* faccenda; *(love ~)* relazione *(f)*
to be afraid of aver paura di
after dopo
afternoon, in the ~ il pomeriggio → p. 14
afterwards poi, dopo
again di nuovo
against contro; **to be ~** essere contrario
age età → p. 9
to agree on mettersi d'accordo su
to agree with essere d'accordo con
aid aiuto; **first ~** pronto soccorso
air aria → p. 16
to be alarmed essere spaventato
all *(adj)* tutto, *(pl)* tutti, tutte, *(adv)* interamente, completamente
to allow permettere
alone solo
along lungo
already già
also anche
to alter cambiare, modificare
always sempre
ambulance autoambulanza
America America
American Americano
among tra, fra
amount somma, importo → p. 70

and e
angry arrabbiato
to be angry (about/at) arrabbiarsi (per)
animal animale *(m)*
annoying seccante, irritante
to answer rispondere
anybody qualcuno
anything qualcosa
to apologize scusarsi → p. 9
appetite appetito
appointment appuntamento → p. 10
area regione *(f)*, luogo
around *(place)* intorno a; *(time)* circa
arrival arrivo → p. 27
to arrive arrivare → p. 27
as *(because)* visto che, siccome; *(way, manner: also prep)* come
to ask *(inquire)* domandare; *(request)* chiedere
to assault attaccare
at once subito
to attack attaccare, aggredire
attention! attenzione!
aunt zia
authorities autorità pubblica
available disponibile
average, on average *(adj)* medio; *(adv)* in media
awake sveglio
away *(to be ~)* essere via; *(far ~)* lontano
awful terribile

B

baby bambino → p. 67
bachelor scapolo, celibe
back *(of person)* schiena; *(opp. of front)* dietro
bad cattivo, *(weather, news)* brutto
badly male
to bandage fasciare → p. 74
band banda (musicale) → p. 61
bank *(finance)* banca → p. 70; *(of river ...)* sponda, riva
barber barbiere *(m)* → p. 50
bar il bar → p. 61
bay golfo

to be *(to exist)* essere; *(place)* trovarsi
to be there essere presente
beach spiaggia → p. 66
beautiful bello
because of a causa di, per
because perché
to become diventare
bed letto → p. 56
bee ape *(f)*
before prima; *(prep)* prima di
to begin iniziare
beginning inizio
behind dietro
to believe credere
bell campanello → p. 22
to belong to appartenere
below sotto
bend curva → p. 22
besides inoltre
beside vicino a
between tra, fra
bicycle bicicletta → p. 17
big grande; *(tall)* alto
bike bicicletta → p. 17
bill conto → p. 33
birthday compleanno → p. 11
birth nascita
a bit un po'
to bite mordere
black nero
blanket coperta
blood il sangue → p. 74
blue blu
board, full ~ pensione completa → p. 55
boat barca → p. 64
body corpo → p. 74
to boil *(water)* bollire
book libro
booking la prenotazione → p. 25, 28; preavviso → p. 59
border frontiera, confine *(m)* → p. 71
boring noioso
born nato
to borrow farsi prestare (da), prendere in prestito (da) → p. 60, 64
boss capo
both tutti e due
to bother disturbare
bottle bottiglia
box office cassa → p. 62, 66
boy ragazzo
brake freno → p. 18
brand marca
to break rompere
to break into/open forzare, scassinare → p. 79
breakdown guasto → p. 18, 22
breakfast la prima colazione → p. 35, 56
bright chiaro; *(weather)* sereno → p. 16
to bring portare (con sè)
brink orlo
to broadcast trasmettere
broad largo
broken guasto, rotto
brother fratello
brother-in-law cognato
building edificio → p. 29
bunch (of flowers) mazzo
bureau de change cambio → p. 70
to burn bruciare
business affare *(m)*

but ma
to buy comprare, fare la spesa → p. 43
by *(close to)* vicino a; *(via, through)* per; *(cause)* da; *(by means of)* per, con
'bye ciao

C

cabin cabina → p. 28
café caffè *(m)*
to calculate calcolare
calendar of events calendario delle manifestazioni → p. 62
to call chiamare, telefonare
call (phone) telefonata → p. 81
to be called chiamarsi, significare
calm *(noun)* calma, pace *(f)*; *(adj.)* calmo, tranquillo; *(weather)* sereno
to calm down calmarsi
camping camping *m*, campeggio → p. 59
canal canale *(m)*
to cancel annullare, disdire → p. 24
car auto *f*, macchina → p. 17
car documents i documenti → p. 23
to carry portare
castle castello → p. 29
cat gatto
cause causa; *(reason)* motivo
caution precauzione *(f)*
celebration festa
centre centro
certain(ly) *(adj)* certo; *(adv)* certamente
to certify certificare
chair sedia
to change modificare; *(money)* cambiare → p. 70; *(clothes)* cambiarsi; **to change the booking** cambiare il biglietto → p. 24
change gli spiccioli, moneta → p. 70
channel canale *(m)*
chapel cappella → p. 30
characteristic qualità
charge *(fee)* tariffa → p. 80, 82
cheap non caro, economico, a buon mercato
to cheat ingannare
to check verificare, controllare
cheeky sfacciato
cheerful allegro
chemist's *(for prescriptions)* farmacia → p. 44; *(for toileteries)* profumeria → p. 46
cheque assegno → p. 70, 79
child bambino → p. 67
to choose scegliere
church chiesa → p. 30
cigarette sigaretta → p. 54
cinema il cinema → p. 62
city centre centro → p. 30
to clean pulire → p. 57
clean pulito
clever intelligente
cliff roccia
climate clima *(m)* → p. 16
to climb salire
clock orologio
close vicino
to close chiudere
closed chiuso
clothing abbigliamento → p. 47
coal carbone *(m)*

ENGLISH-ITALIAN DICTIONARY

coast costa → p. 28
coffee caffè *(m)* → p. 26, 35, 42
coin moneta → p. 71
cold freddo → p. 16, 33
to be cold aver freddo
to collect raccogliere
colour tinta, il colore
to come venire; to come back ritornare; to come from derivare, provenire, discendere; to come in entrare, venire dentro; come in! avanti!
common *(adj)* comune
company compagnia; *(commercial)* società, associazione *(f)*
compass bussola
compensation indennizzo, risarcimento (dei danni)
to complain imprecare, sgridare; to complain (about) reclamare (per) → p. 32, 56; to complain (of/about) lamentarsi (di)
complaint reclamo → p. 32, 56
complete completo, finito
completely interamente, completamente
concert concerto → p. 62
condolence(s) condoglianze *(pl)*
condom preservativo, profilattico
to confirm confermare
to confiscate sequestrare → p. 79
to congratulate congratularsi, fare gli auguri
congratulations augurio → p. 11
connection *(relationship)* rapporto, contatto; *(elec., tele etc.)* comunicazione *(f)* → p. 81, 82, *(train)* coincidenza → p. 25
to connect *(tele)* mettere in comunicazione → p. 81
constitution costituzione *(f)*
consulate consolato
contact contatto
contents contenuto
to continue continuare
contraceptive anticoncezionale *(m)*
contract contratto
contrary contrario
conversation conversazione *(f)*
to cook cucinare
cool fresco
corner angolo
corridor corridoio
corrupt corrotto
to cost costare
cottage villetta, cottage
counter *(bank, post office ...)* sportello
country paese *(m)*
countryside paesaggio → p. 30
couple, married ~ coniugi *(pl)*
course corso; *(meal)* portata, piatto → p. 35
court *(law)* tribunale → p. 79
cousin cugino/cugina
credit card carta di credito → p. 43, 71
to criticize criticare
to cross attraversare
crowded pieno, affolato
to cry piangere
culture cultura → p. 29
curious curioso
currency valuta → p. 71
current *(el)* corrente *(f)* (elettrica)
cushion cuscino
customs dogana, ufficio doganale → p. 71
to cut tagliare

cutlery le posate → p. 33
to cycle andare in bicicletta → p. 17, 64

D

to damage nuocere, danneggiare
damages risarcimento dei danni
damp umido
to dance ballare → p. 61
dangerous pericoloso
dark scuro
date data → p. 14; *(appointment)* appuntamento → p. 10; date of birth data di nascita → p. 71
daughter figlia
day giorno; day of arrival giorno d'arrivo → p. 58
dead morto
deadline termine *(m)*, data; *(period of time)* scadenza
dear caro
death morte *(f)*
debt debito
to decide decidere
decision risoluzione *(f)*, decisione *(f)*
to declare dichiarare
to decline rifiutare
deep profondo
definite definitivo
definitely definitivamente
degree grado
to demand esigere, richiedere
denomination *(rel)* la confessione
dentist dentista → p. 72
department *(shop)* reparto; *(gov)* ministero; *(admin)* sezione *(f)*
departure partenza → p. 26, 57, 78
deposit deposito, acconto
destination destinazione *(f)*
to destroy distruggere
to develop sviluppare
to dial formare il numero → p. 82
to die morire
difference differenza
different(ly) *(adj)* diverso; *(adv)* diversamente
difficult difficile
direction direzione *(f)*
director direttore *(m)*
directory elenco
dirt sporcizia
dirty sporco
disappointed deluso
discotheque discoteca → p. 61
discount sconto
to discover scoprire
dish pietanza, piatto → p. 31
distance distanza
distant lontano
district regione *(f)*, luogo
to distrust diffidare (di qc, qlc), non fidarsi (di qc, qlc)
to disturb disturbare
disturbance disturbo; *(interruption)* interruzione *(f)*
diversion la deviazione → p. 22
to do fare → p. 84
doctor medico → p. 72; *(university degree)* dottore *(m)*
documents i documenti → p. 23, 80

dog cane (m)
door porta; (front ~) portone (m)
double (adj) doppio
to doubt s. th. dubitare di qc
down in giù
to dream sognare
dress vestito → p.47
to dress vestire; (to get dressed) vestirsi; (salad) condire → p.31; (wound) fasciare → p.75
to drink bere → p.31
drink bevanda → p.41, 49
drinking-water acqua potabile → p.60
to drive guidare
driving-licence la patente → p.71
drunk ubriaco, brillo; (tipsy) un po' allegro
dry land terraferma → p.28
duration durata
during durante
duty dovere (m); (tax) i diritti doganali (pl) → p.71

E

early presto
to earn guadagnare
earth terra
east est (m)
easy facile
to eat mangiare → p.31, 49
edge orlo
edible commestibile
education educazione (f), istruzione (f)
effort sforzo
egg uovo → p.39
Eire Repubblica d'Irlanda
either ... or o ... o ...
electrician l'elettricista m → p.47
embassy ambasciata
to embrace abbracciare
emergency brake freno d'emergenza → p.27
emergency exit uscita d'emergenza → p.25
emergency telephone telefono d'emergenza → p.23
empty vuoto
to end finire
engaged (telephone, toilet) occupato; (~ to be married) fidanzato
engine il motore → p.18
England Inghilterra
English inglese
Englishman/-woman inglese
to enjoy godere
enough abbastanza, sufficiente
to enter (the country) entrare (in un paese) → p.72
entertainment divertimento → p.61
entire tutto, completo
entirely interamente, completamente
entrance ingresso
environment ambiente (m)
Europe Europa
European europeo/europea
even (equal amount) uguale; (numbers) pari; (adv) perfino; not ~ nemmeno
evening sera
event avvenimento → p.62; manifestazione (f); (performance) spettacolo → p.62
every (adj) ogni
everybody ognuno

everything tutto
every time ogni volta
everywhere dappertutto
evil cattivo
exact esatto, preciso
exactly precisamente
examination l'esame m → p.75
to examine controllare
example esempio
except eccetto, tranne
to exchange cambiare
exchange cambio → p.70
exchange rate cambio → p.71
excursion gita → p.30
excuse scusa → p.9
exhibition mostra, fiera
exit uscita
expenses spese (pl)
expensive caro
experienced esperto
to expire scadere
to explain spiegare
to extend allungare; (time) prolungare
to extinguish spegnere
to extract tirare → p.77

F

factory fabbrica
fair (just) giusto; (~ haired) biondo; (trade ~) fiera
faith fede (f)
faithful fedele
to fall cadere
false falso
family famiglia
far lontano
fashion moda → p.47
fast (adj) rapido, veloce; (adv) presto, rapidamente, velocemente, in fretta
fat grosso, spesso; (person) grasso
father padre (m)
fault errore, difetto → p.23
fear paura
to fear temere
fee onorario, pagamento → p.80, 82
feeble debole
to feel sentire
feeling sentimento
female (noun) femmina
feminine (adj) femminile
few pochi (m), poche (f)
fiancé/fiancée fidanzato/fidanzata
field campo
to fill in compilare → p.80
filling station stazione di servizio → p.17
film pellicola → p.53
finally finalmente
to find trovare; to find out venire a sapere
fine (penalty) multa; (well) molto bene; (weather) bello
to finish finire; finished finito
fire fuoco; fire brigade vigili (pl) del fuoco, pompieri (pl); fire extinguisher estintore (m)
firm ditta
first name il nome → p.72
first of all prima
fish pesce (m) → p.38

ENGLISH-ITALIAN DICTIONARY

flash *(photo)* flash *(m)* → p. 53
flat *(apartment)* appartamento; *(adj)* piano, piatto
flight volo → p. 24
to flirt flirt → p. 10
floor pavimento; *(storey)* piano
to flow scorrere
flower fiore *(m)*
fly mosca
to fly volare
to follow seguire
food alimentari *(pl)* → p. 31, 33, 49
for per
to forbid proibire
foreign straniero
foreigner straniero
forest bosco → p. 30
to forget dimenticare
to forgive scusare, perdonare
fork forchetta
form formulario, modulo → p. 71, 80
fragile fragile
free libero; *(of charge)* gratuito, gratis
to freeze gelare
French francese
frequently *(adv)* spesso
fresh fresco; *(linen)* pulito
friend (boy~/girl~) amico/amica
friendly amichevole
to frighten spaventare
from da, di
in front of davanti a
fruit la frutta → p. 40
full pieno, completo; *(full up)* sazio
full board pensione completa → p. 56
fun *(enjoyment)* divertimento
funny divertente, comico
furious arrabbiato, furioso
furniture mobile *(m)*
fuse fusibile → p. 23

G

to gain guadagnare, ottenere
garage garage *(m)* → p. 18
garden giardino
gear *(car)* marcia → p. 23
gentleman signore
genuine vero, autentico
to get procurare, provvedere; ricevere; *(obtain)* ottenere; **to get drunk** ubriacarsi; **to get engaged to** fidanzarsi con; **to get off** scendere → p. 27, 78; **to get to know s. o.** conoscere qlc, fare la conoscenza di qlc → p. 8; **to get up** alzarsi
gift regalo
girl ragazza
to give dare; **to give as a present** regalare
glad contento, felice
gladly volentieri
glad (about) lieto (di)
glass *(pane of ~)* vetro; *(drinking ~)* bicchiere *(m)* → p. 33
glasses occhiali *(pl)* → p. 52
gnat zanzara
to go *(by train, car etc.)* andare; **to go away** andar via; **to go for a walk** passeggiare; **to go shopping** fare la spesa → p. 43
God Dio

good *(adj)* buono; *(adv)* bene
goodbye! arrivederci! → p. 11; **to say goodbye** congedarsi, accomiatarsi
government governo
grandfather nonno
grandmother nonna
grandson/granddaughter nipote *(m, f)*
grass erba
grave tomba
great grande
green verde
to greet salutare → p. 8
grey grigio
ground suolo; **ground-floor** pianoterra, pianterreno
group gruppo
guarantee garanzia
to guess indovinare
guest ospite *(m)*
guest house la pensione → p. 55
guide guida *(m, f)* (turistica) → p. 54, il cicerone → p. 30
guided tour visita guidata → p. 29
guilt colpa
guitar chitarra

H

hair i capelli → p. 46, 50
hairdresser's il parrucchiere → p. 50
half mezzo
hall *(entrance)* ingresso; *(room)* sala
halt! alt!
to happen accadere, succedere
happy contento, felice, allegro
to harass infastidire → p. 80
hard duro
hardly appena
to harm nuocere, danneggiare
harmful dannoso
to have avere → p. 84; **to have to** dovere; **to have a look** dare un' occhiata
he lui, egli
head testa, capo
health salute *(f)*
healthy sano
to hear udire, sentire
heating riscaldamento → p. 23, 56
heaven cielo
heavy pesante
height altezza
hello buon giorno; *(hi)* ciao; *(on the phone)* pronto
help aiuto
her *(possessive pronoun, f)* (il) suo, (la) sua
here qui
high alto
to hike fare un escursione a piedi → p. 65
hill collina
to hire noleggiare → p. 60, 64
his *(possessive pronoun)* (il) suo, (la) sua
history storia
hobby hobby *(m)*
hole buco
holiday vacanza, giorno festivo → p. 15
holidays ferie *(pl)*; **holiday home** casa per le vacanze → p. 58
holy santo
at home a casa

to hope sperare
hospital l'ospedale *m* → p. 74, 75
host/hostess ospite *(m, f)*, padrone/padrona di casa
hot caldo → p. 16, 34
hotel hotel *(m)* → p. 55
hour ora → p. 13; **hours of business** orari d'apertura
house casa
household goods articoli casalinghi → p. 51
how? come?
however però, comunque, tuttavia
to hug abbracciare
hunger fame *(f)*
hungry affamato
to hurt far male → p. 76
husband marito
hut capanna; *(mountain ~)* baita

I

I io
idea idea
identity card carta d'identità → p. 72, 79
if se
ill malato → p. 72
illness malattia → p. 72
immediately subito
impolite scortese
import importazione *(f)* → p. 72
important importante
impossible impossibile
in in; **in front of** davanti a
included compreso
to inform avvertire; informare
information informazioni *(f)* → p. 17, 24, 26
inhabitant abitante *(f, m)*
inn locanda
innocent innocente
to inquire informarsi
insect insetto
inside dentro
instead of invece di
to insult offendere
insurance assicurazione *(f)*
intelligent intelligente
to be interested (in) interessarsi (di)
international internazionale
to interrupt interrompere
interruption l'interruzione *(f)*
introduction presentazione *(f)* → p. 8
invalid *(document)* non valido; *(sick person)* infermo
to invite invitare
Ireland Irlanda
Irishman/-woman irlandese
island isola
isolated solo, solitario
Italy Italia
Italian italiano/italiana
its *(possessive pronoun)* (il) suo, la sua
item articolo; *(on agenda)* argomento

J

jewellery gioielli → p. 52
job lavoro, posto, impiego
joke scherzo

journey viaggio
joy gioia
to judge giudicare

K

to keep tenere
key la chiave → p. 56, 57, 79
kind *(adj)* gentile
kind *(type)* tipo, genere
kindness gentilezza, cortesia
to kiss baciare
kiss bacio
kitchen cucina
knife coltello
to know conoscere; *(facts)*sapere

L

lack mancanza
to lack mancare
lady signora
lake lago
land terra
landlord/landlady proprietario/a → p. 59
language lingua
large grande
to last durare
last *(adj)* ultimo/ultima
late tardi; **to be late** ritardare
later più tardi
to laugh ridere
lavatory toilette *(f)*, gabinetto → p. 56, 58, 59
lazy pigro
to learn imparare
at least almeno
to leave lasciare; *(go away)* andar via; **to leave (for)** partire (per)
left, on the ~, to the ~ a sinistra
to lend prestare → p. 60, 64
length lunghezza
less (di) meno
to let *(allow)* permettere; *(rent)* affittare → p. 19, 58, 59
letter lettera → p. 80
lie *(untruth)* menzogna, bugia
to lie *(to tell lies)* mentire
to lie down sdraiarsi
life vita
lifeboat scialuppa di salvataggio → p. 28
lift ascensore *(m)*
light *(noun)* luce *(f)*
light *(not heavy)* leggero
lightning fulmine *(m)* → p. 16
like *(similar to)* come
to like piacere; *(to want)* volere
line *(telephone, rail)* linea → p. 81, 82
to listen to ascoltare
little piccolo; **a little** un po'
to live vivere; *(reside)* abitare
location posizione *(f)*
to lock (up) chiudere a chiave
lonely solo, solitario
long lungo
long-distance call interurbana → p. 82
to look guardare; **to look after** occuparsi di; **to look for** cercare; **to look forward to** rallegrarsi di; **look out!** attenzione!

ENGLISH-ITALIAN DICTIONARY

lorry il camion
to lose perdere → p. 65, 80; **to lose one's way** smarrirsi, perdersi
loss perdita
lost, to get ~ smarrirsi, perdersi
lost-property office ufficio oggetti smarriti → p. 78
a lot of molto
loud rumoroso
loudspeaker altoparlante *(m)*
to love amare
low basso
low season bassa stagione *f* → p. 57
luck fortuna
lucky felice, fortunato
luggage bagaglio → p. 25
lunch pranzo → p. 31

M

machine macchina
madam, Mrs signora
magazine rivista → p. 54
maiden name il nome da ragazza → p. 72
mainland terraferma → p. 28
to make fare, produrre; **to make a phone call** telefonare → p. 81; **to make up one's mind** decidersi
male *(noun)* maschio
male *(adj)* maschile
man uomo
manager direttore *(m)*
map carta geografica → p. 54; **map of walks** mappa dei sentieri → p. 54
market mercato → p. 30, 49
married to sposato con → p. 72
to marry sposare
mass messa
material stoffa
matter *(affair)* faccenda, questione *(f)*; **what's the** ~? cosa c'è?
maybe forse
me, to me mi, a me
meadow prato
meal pasto → p. 31
mean cattivo
to mean significare
meat carne *(f)* → p. 37
medicine medicina, farmaco → p. 44
to meet incontrare; **to meet again** rivedere
menu il menu → p. 31, 35
merry allegro
message messagio
middle mezzo, centro
minus meno
minute minuto
misfortune sfortuna, disgrazia
to miss *(to be too late)* perdere
missing *(lost)* smarrito; **to be missing** mancare
Miss signorina
mistake errore *(m)*, sbaglio; **by mistake** erroneamente, per sbaglio; **to mistake for** scambiare; **to be mistaken** sbagliarsi
to misunderstand fraintendere
mixed misto
modern moderno
moist umido
moment momento, istante *(m)*
money denaro, soldi → p. 70, 80

month mese *(m)* → p. 15
moon luna
more più
morning, during the ~ la mattina → p. 14
mosquito zanzara
mother madre *(f)*
motive motivo, ragione *(f)*
motor il motore → p. 18
motorbike motocicletta → p. 17
mountain montagna, **mountains** montagne → p. 30
to move *(s. th.)* muovere, spostare; *(to ~ house)* cambiare casa
movie film *(m)* → p. 62
Mr signor
much molto
mud fango
to mug *(attack)* attaccare, aggredire
museum museo → p. 29
music musica
my (il) mio

N

naked nudo
name nome *(m)* → p. 8, 72, **first** ~ il nome → p. 72
national code prefisso → p. 81
nationality nazionalità → p. 72
native country patria
nature natura
naughty cattivo
nausea nausea → p. 76
near vicino (a)
necessary necessario
to need aver bisogno di
neighbour vicino/vicina
nephew nipote *(m)*
nervous nervoso → p. 76
never mai
nevertheless ciò nonostante, tuttavia
new nuovo
news novità, notizie
newspaper giornale *(m)* → p. 44, 54
next prossimo; **next to** vicino a
nice simpatico, gentile
niece nipote *(f)*
night notte *(f)* → p. 14; **night-club** il night-club → p. 61
nobody nessuno
noise rumore *(m)*, chiasso
noisy rumoroso
noon mezzogiorno
normal normale
north nord *(m)*
Northern Ireland Irlanda del Nord
not non
nothing niente
now ora → p. 14
nowhere in nessun luogo, da nessuna parte
nude nudo
number numero → *see inside front cover*
nurse infermiera

O

object oggetto
occasion occasione *(f)*

ocean oceano
of di, da
of course naturalmente
to offend offendere
to offer offrire
office ufficio
often spesso
oil olio → p. 23, 34
old vecchio; *(ancient, antique)* antico
on su; **on the right** a destra; **on top of** sopra;
on the way per la strada → p. 17; **on time**
(adj) puntuale, *(adv)* puntualmente
once una volta; **at ~** subito
one un/uno/una
only *(adj)* solo, unico; *(adv)* solo, soltanto,
solamente
open aperto
to open aprire
opening hours orari d'apertura
opinion opinione
opportunity occasione *(f)*
opposite contrario; opposto
or o, oppure
order l'ordinazione *f* → p. 31
order, out of ~ rotto, guasto
organs organi → p. 74
other, the ~ l'altro
our (il) nostro, (la) nostra
outside fuori
over *(above)* sopra, su; *(finished)* passato
overseas oltremare *(m)*
to overtake sorpassare
to owe dovere
to own possedere
owner proprietario

P

to pack *(bags)* fare le valigie
package pacchetto
page pagina
pain dolore *(m)*
to be painful far male → p. 76
painting quadro
a pair of un paio di
papers i documenti → p. 23, 80
parcel pacco → p. 81
pardon? come?, scusi? → p. 7, 9
parents genitori *(pl)*
to park parcheggiare → p. 18
park parco, giardino pubblico
part parte *(f)*
particulars generalità *(pl)*
party festa
pass *(in mountains)* passo
passage transito, passaggio
passenger passeggero → p. 25, 28
passing through di passaggio
passport passaporto → p. 80, 72
passport control controllo passaporti → p. 71
past *(in front of)* davanti; *(relating to time)*
passato
path sentiero
to pay pagare; **to pay attention to** stare attento a; **to pay duty on** *(to clear through customs)* sdoganare
payment pagamento → p. 71
peace pace *(f)*
people gente *(f)*; *(nation)* popolo

per a, per
percent percento
performance *(theatre)* rappresentazione *(f)*,
spettacolo → p. 8, 62
perhaps forse, magari
permission permesso
to permit permettere
person persona
to perspire sudare
petrol benzina → p. 17
petrol station stazione di servizio → p. 17
to phone telefonare → p. 81
photo, to take a ~ fotografare
photo(graph) foto *(f)*, fotografia → p. 53
photographic materials gli articoli fotografici
→ p. 53
picture quadro
piece pezzo
pillow cuscino
pity, it's a ~ è un peccato
place luogo → p. 12; *(seat)* posto → p. 30;
place of birth luogo di nascita → p. 72
plain pianura
plane → p. aereo → p. 24
plant pianta
to play *(game)* giocare; *(instrument)* suonare
to please piacere
please prego; per favore → p. 7, 9
pleased (with) lieto (di)
pleasure gioia, piacere *(m)* → p. 61
plus più
poison veleno
poisoning avvelenamento → p. 76
police polizia → p. 79
polite cortese
politics politica
poor povero
port porto → p. 27
porter il portiere → p. 57
position posizione *(f)*, situazione *(f)*; *(post)*
impiego
possible possibile
to post imbucare → p. 81
post office ufficio postale → p. 80
to postpone rimandare, rinviare
pot *(cooking ~)* pentola
pottery ceramica
prayer preghiera
to prefer preferire
pregnant incinta, gravida
to prescribe prescrivere → p. 76
present *(gift)* regalo
to be present essere presente
pretty grazioso/a, bellino/a
price prezzo
priest prete *(m)*
prison la prigione → p. 80
prize premio
probable probabile
probably probabilmente
problem questione *(f)*, problema *(m)*
profession professione *(f)*
programme programma *(m)* → p. 65, *(radio,
TV)* trasmissione *(f)*
prohibited vietato
promise promessa
to pronounce pronunciare
proper *(correct)* giusto; *(suitable)* adatto
protection protezione *(f)*
pub bar, osteria, trattoria → p. 61

ENGLISH-ITALIAN DICTIONARY

public pubblico
public transport trasporti pubblici → p. 77
to pull tirare → p. 77
punctual (adj) puntuale
punishment punizione (f), castigo; (penalty) pena
purchase compera
purse portamonete (m)
to push spingere
to put (down) mettere (giú); to put off rimandare; to put out (cigarette, light) spegnere

Q

quality qualità
question domanda; (issue) questione (f), problema (m)
quick rapido, svelto, veloce
quickly presto, rapidamente, velocemente, in fretta
quiet silenzioso, piano, a bassa voce; tranquillo
quite (completely) proprio, perfettamente; (rather) abbastanza

R

radio radio (f) → p. 57
railway ferrovia → p. 26
to rain piovere → p. 16
rape violenza(carnale), stupro → p. 80
rare (adj) raro; (adv) raramente
rather (adv) piuttosto
to reach raggiungere
to read leggere
ready pronto
to realize rendersi conto di; (understand) capire
really (adv) assolutamente
reason ragione (f), motivo
receipt, to give a ~ dare la ricevuta
to receive ricevere
recently recentemente → p. 14
reception ricevimento; (hospital, doctor) l'accettazione f → p. 72, (hotel) la reception → p. 55
to recognize riconoscere
to recommend raccomandare
to recover rimettersi
red rosso
reduction riduzione (f) → p. 26
to refuse (s. th.) rifiutare; (to do s.th.) rifiutarsi (di fare qc)
region regione (f), luogo
to register consegnare → p. 26
registration registrazione f → p. 58; ~ number targa
related imparentato
religion religione (f)
reluctantly malvolentieri
to remain rimanere
remedy rimedio → p. 44
to remember ricordarsi
to remember s. th. tenere a mente qc
to remind s. o. of s. th. ricordare a qlc qc
to rent affittare → p. 19, 58, 59
rent pigione (f), affitto → p. 59
repair riparazione (f) → p. 18
to repeat ripetere

to replace sostituire
to reply rispondere
request domanda → p. 7, 9
reservation la prenotazione → p. 27, 55
residence, place of residence domicilio, residenza → p. 72
responsible responsabile
restaurant ristorante (m) → p. 31
restless irrequieto, agitato
rest riposo; (remainder) resto
to rest riposarsi
result risultato → p. 65
to return ritornare
return ritorno
reward ricompensa
rich ricco
right giusto; (suitable) adatto; (on the ~) destra; to be right aver ragione
to ring suonare
to ring (up) telefonare → p. 81
risk rischio
river fiume (m)
road via, strada; (country ~) strada provinciale → p. 24, 78; road map carta automobilistica → p. 24, 54
rock roccia
(roll of) film pellicola → p. 53
room camera → p. 55
rotten (food) marcio
round rotondo
route itinerario
row (line) fila
rubbish immondizia → p. 59
rude sgarbato
rule regolamento
to run correre

S

sad triste
safe (adj) sicuro; (adv) certamente
safety sicurezza
sale vendita
same uguale; the same lo stesso
satisfied contento, soddisfatto
to save salvare
to say dire
scarcely appena
scenery paesaggio → p. 30
Scotland Scozia
Scotsman/-woman scozzese
to scream gridare
sea mare (m)
season stagione (f) → p. 15
seat posto → p. 30
secluded isolato
second secondo
secret segreto
security sicurezza
to see again rivedere
to see vedere
seldom (adv) raramente
self-service shop il self-service → p. 44
to send inviare, mandare
sender il mittente → p. 81
sentence frase (f)
separate separato
serious serio; (injury) grave
to serve servire

service servizio; *(church)* messa, la funzione sacra → p. 30
services la stazione di servizio, posto di ristoro → p. 24
to set *(to place, to put)* mettere
to settle sistemare
sex sesso
shade *(colour)* tono, tonalità
she ella, lei
ship la nave → p. 27
shoe scarpa → p. 53
shop negozio → p. 43
shore sponda
short *(length, distance)* corto; *(time)* breve
shortage mancanza
shot colpo
to shout gridare
to show mostrare; *(indicate)* indicare
to shut chiudere
shut chiuso
shy timido
Sicily Sicilia
sick malato → p. 72
side parte *(f)*, lato
sightseeing tour of the town/city giro della città → p. 29
sights le cose da vedersi, attrazioni turistiche → p. 29
signature firma → p. 70
sign segno, indizio; *(road ~)* segnale *(m)* → p. 24; *(shop ~)* insegna; *(notice)* avviso
silence silenzio
silent silenzioso; tranquillo; **to be silent** tacere
since *(time)* da; *(because)* siccome
to sing cantare
single *(man)* celibe; *(woman)* nubile → p. 72
sister-in-law cognata
sister sorella; *(nurse)* infermiera; *(nun)* suora
to sit sedere
situation situazione *(f)*
size *(dimension)* grandezza; *(clothes, shoes)* misura
sky cielo
to sleep dormire
slender snello
slight lieve
slim snello, magro
slow lento; **slowly** lentamente, piano
small piccolo
smell odore *(m)*
to smell sentire
to smoke fumare
smoker fumatore → p. 25
smooth piano, liscio
to smuggle fare contrabbando
snack spuntino
to snow nevicare
society società, associazione *(f)*, compagnia
so così
soft morbido; *(colour, light)* tenue
solid solido, duro
some alcuni, alcune
somebody qualcuno
something qualcosa
sometimes a volte → p. 14
son figlio
song canzone *(f)*
soon presto → p. 14
to be sorry dispiacersi; **I'm sorry** mi dispiace

sort specie *(f)*, genere, tipo
sound suono, rumore
source *(of river)* sorgente *(f)*, fonte *(f)*
south sud *(m)*
space spazio
to speak parlare
speed velocità
spend the night pernottare → p. 55
spoiled rovinato
spoon cucchiaio
sport sport *(m)* → p. 63
spot *(place)* luogo, posto → p. 12
spring *(source)* sorgente *(f)*, fonte *(f)*
square piazza → p. 12
staff personale *(m)*
staircase scala
stairs scala
stamp francobollo → p. 80, 81
to stamp *(letter)* affrancare → p. 80, 81
to stand stare (in piedi)
star stella
to start iniziare
to startle spaventare
state *(pol.)* Stato *(m)*
stationery articoli di cartoleria → p. 54
station la stazione → p. 26
to stay rimanere; *(the night)* pernottare → p. 55
to steal rubare
steep ripido
steps scala
still *(adj)* silenzioso, calmo
still *(adv)* ancora
to sting pungere, pizzicare
stone pietra
stop *(bus, train)* fermata → p. 27, 77; **stop!** alt!
to stop fermare, fermarsi, smettere
story storia
stout *(person)* grasso
stove stufa
straight on diritto
strange strano
stranger sconosciuto
street via, strada; *(main road)* strada principale → p. 24, 78
strenuous faticoso
to study studiare
stupid stupido, scemo
style lo stile
suburb sobborgo
subway sottopassaggio
success successo, riuscita
suddenly all'improvviso, di colpo
sufficient sufficiente
suitcase valigia
summit cima, punta
sum somma, importo
sun sole *(m)* → p. 16
sunglasses occhiali da sole *(pl)*
sunny soleggiato, assolato → p. 16
supermarket supermercato → p. 44
supplement supplemento → p. 27
sure *(adj)* sicuro; *(adv)* certamente
surname il cognome → p. 72
surprised sorpreso
to swap scambiare
to sweat sudare
to swim nuotare → p. 66
swimming pool piscina → p. 66
switch interruttore *(m)*

94

T

table tavolo, tavola
to take prendere; *(time)* durare; *(train ...)* prendere → p. 24, 26, 27, 77; *(to carry)* portare; *(~ away)* portar via; **to take care of** occuparsi di, stare attento (a); **to take out** tirare → p. 77; **to take part (in)** prendere parte (a); **to take place** aver luogo; **to take a photo** fotografare → p. 53
take-off decollo → p. 24
talk conversazione *(f)*
to talk discorrere, parlare
tall alto
taste gusto, sapore *(m)*
to taste assaggiare
taxi taxi *(m)*; **taxi-driver** tassista *(m/f)* → p. 81
telephone telefono → p. 81
to tell dire, raccontare
temperature temperatura → p. 16
terrible terribile
than di, che
to thank ringraziare → p. 9
thank you! grazie! → p. 7
theatre teatro → p. 62
theft furto → p. 80
their *(possessive pronoun)* (il/la) loro, *(pl)* (i/le) loro
then allora
then *(next)* poi
there là
there is, there are c'è, ci sono
therefore perciò, quindi
they loro
thick grosso, spesso
thing cosa
to think pensare; *(to believe)* credere
thin sottile; *(slim)* snello
thirsty assetato; **I'm thirsty** ho sete
this, these questo/a, questi/e
thought pensiero
through *(place)* attraverso; *(by)* per
thunderstorm temporale *(m)* → p. 16
ticket, admission ~ biglietto → p. 26, 62, 66, 77
ticket office cassa → p. 66, 27, 62
time l'ora, tempo → p. 13, *(occasion)* volta; **in time** *(adv)* a tempo, in tempo
timetable orario → p. 27, 77
tip mancia → p. 34, 81
tired stanco
to a, **to Bologna** a Bologna, *(up to)* fino a
tobacco tabacco → p. 54
today oggi → p. 56
together insieme
toilet toilette *(f)*, gabinetto → p. 56, 58, 59
tomb tomba
tomorrow domani → p. 13
too *(also)* anche
too *(+ adj)* troppo; **too much** troppo
tour visita → p. 29
tourist information office ente *(m)* per il turismo
to tow (away) rimorchiare, trainare → p. 24
towards verso
town città
town centre centro → p. 30
town hall municipio → p. 30

town map pianta della città → p. 54
traffic traffico
train treno → p. 26
to transfer trasferire
transit-visa permesso di transito
to translate tradurre
to travel viaggiare
travel agency agenzia di viaggi → p. 44
traveller's cheque assegno turistico, il traveller's chèque → p. 71
tree albero
trip viaggio, gita → p. 30
trouble problemi, difficoltà
true vero
to try tentare; *(to taste)* assaggiare
tunnel tunnel *(m)*, galleria
type tipo, specie *(f)*
typical tipico, caratteristico

U

ugly brutto
umbrella ombrello → p. 48
uncertain incerto, dubbio
uncle zio
unconscious svenuto, senza conoscenza, privo di sensi → p. 77
under sotto
to understand capire
unfortunately purtroppo
unfriendly antipatico
unhealthy malsano
unkind poco gentile, scortese
unknown sconosciuto
unlucky infelice, sfortunato
until fino a
unwell indisposto
up sù, in alto
urgent urgente
us *(direct, indirect)* ci; **to us** a noi
to use usare

V

vacant libero
in vain invano
valid valido → p. 72
value valore *(m)*
Venice Venezia
versus contro
very (much) molto
view vista → p. 30; *(opinion)* opinione
village villaggio
visa visto → p. 71
visible visibile
to visit visitare → p. 10
voice voce *(f)*
vote voto
to vote votare
voyage viaggio

W

wages paga, salario
to wait aspettare
waiter/waitress il cameriere/la cameriera → p. 31

waiting room sala d'aspetto → p. 27, 77
to wake svegliare
Wales Galles
to walk camminare
wallet portafoglio → p. 79
to want volere
war guerra
warm caldo → p. 16
to warn (of/about) avvertire (di)
to wash lavare
to watch guardare
watch *(wrist~)* orologio
water acqua → p. 34, 58, 60
way via; *(path)* sentiero; *(road, route)* strada
way out uscita
we noi
weak debole
to wear portare
weather tempo → p. 16
wedding nozze *(pl)*, matrimonio
weekdays, on ~ nei giorni feriali
week settimana → p. 14
to weigh pesare
weight peso
to welcome accogliere, ricevere → p. 8
well *(adv)* bene
Welshman/Welshwoman gallese
west ovest; *(the West)* l'Occidente *(m)*
wet bagnato; *(soaked)* inzuppato → p. 16
what cosa, che cosa
when quando
whether se
while mentre

white bianco
whole *(adj)* tutto, intero
why perché
wide largo, ampio
wife moglie *(f)*
to win vincere, guadagnare → p. 66
to wish desiderare; *(to want)* volere
with con
within *(time)* entro → p. 14
without senza
witness testimone *(m)*
woman donna
wood legno; *(fire ~)* legna
woods bosco → p. 30
word parola
to work lavorare; *(machine)* funzionare
world mondo
to be worried about preoccuparsi di
to write scrivere; **in writing** per iscritto
wrong sbagliato; **to be wrong** sbagliarsi

Y

year anno
yellow giallo
yet già, ancora
you tu, *(polite form)* lei; *(pl)* voi, loro → p. 84
young giovane
your *(sing)* (il) tuo, (la) tua; *(pl)* (il) vostro, (la) vostra
youth hostel ostello per la gioventù → p. 60